Wealth

Blacklist

The Hidden Codes the Elites Use to Multiply Money, Control Assets, and Escape Financial Slavery

Staten House

Written in quiet defiance, extracted from the forbidden layers, and offered to those ready to unhook from the system and build what was always theirs.

Table of Contents

PROLOGUE: The Game You Were Never Taught

You were never supposed to question it.

From the moment you entered this world, the rules were already set. You were taught what to believe, what to chase, and how to measure success. You were handed a script that billions follow without ever asking who wrote it.

Go to school.
Get good grades.
Find a stable job.
Work hard.
Save a little.
Retire someday if you're lucky.

That's the script.

It was sold to you as the path to security, success, and freedom. But what no one told you is this:

The system was never designed to make you free. It was designed to keep you controlled.

The Invisible Program

From childhood, you were programmed to see money through a narrow lens.
You were taught that money comes from labor — that wealth is earned slowly, painfully, by trading your time for someone else's profit.

You were trained to fear risk.
To see debt as dangerous.
To believe that taxes are unavoidable.

To think that true wealth is only for the lucky few who somehow "made it."

What you weren't shown is that **the people who control the system never followed that script themselves.**

The ultra-wealthy play by entirely different rules — rules you were never allowed to see.
They don't trade time for money.
They don't chase job security.
They don't fear debt — they use it as fuel.
They don't get crushed by taxes — they legally avoid them.
They don't work harder — they build systems.

And while you were taught to chase stability, they were busy acquiring control.

The Two Financial Games

There are two financial games happening at the same time.

The first game is the one you were taught.
The public game.
The school system, the corporate ladder, the paycheck-to-paycheck struggle, the save-and-retire fantasy.

This is the game designed for the masses.
The hamster wheel that keeps billions trapped, distracted, and obedient.

The second game is the private one.
The hidden game.

This is the game played by the wealthy, the powerful, the untouchables.
It's built on entities, trusts, tax codes, credit leverage, asset protection, and multiplying wealth through systems you were never educated to understand.

And while most people are grinding harder in the public game, a small minority are pulling the real strings in silence.

Why You've Never Seen It

You weren't supposed to.

The education system doesn't teach wealth creation.
The media doesn't expose the wealth codes.
The financial industry profits by keeping you dependent.
And the people who know how the game truly works have every incentive to keep it quiet.

Because once you see it, you can't unsee it.
Once you understand how the rules really work, everything you've been taught begins to crumble.

The truth is brutally simple:

The system is working exactly as it was designed.

It's not broken.
It's not failing.
It's performing perfectly — for those it was built to serve.

Why This Book Exists

This is not a book about motivation.
This is not a book about working harder.
This is not a book about budgeting your coffee or sacrificing for 40 years in hopes of retirement.

This is your entry point into the hidden game.

Inside these pages, you will see:

- The forbidden codes the elites quietly use.

- How wealth is multiplied and protected far outside the systems you were taught.

- How debt, taxes, and credit are used as tools — not traps.

- How entities, structures, and legal shields are built to protect assets.

- How stealth wealth allows you to build quietly while remaining invisible.

You don't need to become someone different.
You need to learn what was hidden from you.

Welcome to the game you were never taught.
It starts now.

PART I — THE LIE

Chapter 1: The Wealth Trap

The Illusion of Success: Why Working Hard Keeps You Stuck

You were taught that hard work is the key.

Work harder than everyone else.
Sacrifice more.
Wake up earlier.
Grind longer.
And one day, you'll finally "make it."

That's the lie most people live their entire lives believing.

But the truth is brutal:

Hard work alone was never designed to make you rich.

The Lie You Were Sold

From childhood, you were programmed to equate effort with success.
The school system drilled it into you: study hard, get good grades, get a job, climb the ladder, and eventually, you'll be rewarded.

But if hard work truly created wealth, then the hardest-working people would be the richest.
The single mother working two jobs.
The laborer grinding 60 hours a week.
The nurse pulling endless night shifts.
The truck driver running nonstop routes.

These people work harder than most CEOs.

Yet, they struggle to pay bills while those at the top accumulate more wealth than entire cities.

The gap is not because of effort.
The gap is because of leverage.

Why The System Loves Hard Workers

The system doesn't want you lazy — it wants you obedient.
A hard worker who believes the system works is easy to control.

You'll take on debt to fund your education.
You'll chase promotions inside corporations you don't own.
You'll pay taxes automatically every paycheck.
You'll save money in accounts that lose value every year to inflation.
You'll be praised for your work ethic while being quietly drained.

The system rewards you with small raises, titles, and temporary comfort to keep you grinding — but never fully free.

Because a worker chasing stability rarely questions who actually controls the system they're working inside.

The Real Currency: Ownership

The wealthy don't trade time for money.
They build and control systems that make money whether they work or not.

- They own businesses, not jobs.

- They control assets that generate cash flow: real estate, investments, intellectual property.

- They use leverage — money, credit, tax strategies, and legal entities — to multiply wealth far beyond what labor could ever produce.

They understand what most were never taught:

You can work hard for 40 years, or you can build systems that work for you 24/7.

The wealthiest people often work far less than the middle class.
Not because they're lazy — but because they learned early that effort is a limited resource.
Systems, capital, and leverage have no such limit.

Why Hard Work Feels Safer

For most people, hard work feels noble.
It feels safe.
It gives a sense of control — as if effort alone can eventually force success.

This is exactly why the system promotes it.
Because while you focus on grinding, you remain blind to the real levers of wealth.

Hard work is important — but only when applied to building leverage.

- Building ownership.
- Building assets.
- Building systems.

Without leverage, hard work is just exhaustion disguised as progress.

The Awakening

You were never lazy.
You were simply following a rigged script.

The illusion of success was designed to keep you stuck — endlessly working inside systems you don't own, paying into structures that benefit those above you.

The moment you see it, everything changes.

The first rule of the hidden game is this:
Wealth flows to those who control systems — not to those who trade time for dollars.

In the next sections, you'll learn exactly how the elites build those systems — and how you can begin doing the same.

The Invisible Handcuffs: Systems Designed for Dependency

Most people don't realize they're trapped because the cage was built to feel safe.

You were never physically forced into this system.
You walked into it — because from your earliest days, you were conditioned to believe this was the only path.

But behind the illusion of choice lies something far more sinister:

A network of invisible handcuffs designed to lock you into lifelong financial dependency.

The Debt Chain

It starts before you even enter adulthood.

- You borrow money for education.

- You're told it's an "investment" in your future.

- You graduate burdened with debt — but no assets.

From the beginning, you start in the negative.

The system then pushes you further:

- Car loans.

- Credit cards.

- Mortgages.

- Personal loans.

Each obligation feels like progress — a car to get to work, a home to feel stable, credit to cover emergencies.

But each layer adds another link to your chain:

The more you owe, the less freedom you have.

You work to pay lenders.
You sacrifice choices to meet obligations.
You stay employed because your bills require it.

The debt machine quietly transforms free individuals into obedient workers.

The Tax Extraction

Once you start earning, the system tightens the next set of cuffs: taxes.

- Your income is automatically taxed before you ever see it.

- The more you earn through labor, the higher your tax burden.

- Meanwhile, the wealthy — who earn through assets — pay far less on a percentage basis.

You become the highest taxed class:

The W2 employee — the person trading time for wages.

The tax code quietly punishes those who rely on labor while rewarding those who build businesses, acquire assets, and structure income differently.

The system doesn't just take your labor — it taxes your labor the most heavily.

The Inflation Trap

Even what you manage to save loses value every year.

Inflation silently erodes your purchasing power.
While your savings sit in a bank earning nearly nothing, the cost of living rises, prices inflate, and your dollars buy less and less.

This forces you to keep working harder to maintain the same lifestyle.

And while you're fighting inflation, the elite are investing in assets that rise in value with inflation — real estate, equities, businesses — growing wealth while the working class bleeds purchasing power.

Inflation is not accidental. It's a hidden tax built into the system.

The Employment Illusion

You're told that job security is the key.
The "safe" path.

But true security comes from ownership, not employment.

- You don't control your income.

- You don't control your hours.

- You don't control your future.

One corporate decision, one economic downturn, one policy change —
and everything you built through labor can vanish.

The system makes you believe that obedience equals safety.
In reality, obedience equals dependence.

**The system's greatest achievement is convincing people to
voluntarily stay trapped inside it.**

Dependency Was Engineered

None of this is accidental.

The financial structure you were born into was carefully built to:

- Keep you working.

- Keep you paying.

- Keep you borrowing.

- Keep you dependent.

**Because dependent people don't rebel.
Dependent people don't build power.
Dependent people serve the system.**

Once you recognize how the trap was engineered, you can begin
dismantling it.

The next layer isn't about working harder or making small sacrifices.

It's about breaking free from the programming itself.

Awakening to the Real Game

At some point, the cracks begin to show.

You work harder, but you're not free.
You save more, but you're not secure.
You follow the rules, but the finish line keeps moving.

That's when the question surfaces:

What if the problem isn't me?
What if the problem is the game itself?

The Silent Minority Who Play a Different Game

While billions follow the public script, a small group operates quietly in the shadows — playing an entirely different financial game.

- They don't trade time for money.

- They don't panic over job losses.

- They don't fear debt.

- They don't get crushed by taxes.

Why?
Because they never agreed to play the public game you were taught.

They learned early that true wealth doesn't come from labor — it comes from **leverage, ownership, and control.**

- They control businesses that print money whether they're working or not.

- They acquire assets that appreciate while the masses rent or borrow.

- They structure income streams to reduce or eliminate taxes.

- They borrow money to expand wealth, while others drown in debt.

The rules you were taught were designed for you.
The rules they follow were designed for themselves.

The Architecture of Control

The system is brilliant in its design:

- **Education** trains obedience, not critical thinking.

- **Employment** rewards loyalty, not ownership.

- **Debt** funds consumption, not wealth.

- **Taxes** punish labor, not capital.

- **Inflation** erodes savings, not assets.

And while the masses argue over wages and politics, the elites accumulate silent control:

- Private entities.

- Trust structures.

- International protections.

- Legal tax avoidance.

- Generational wealth transfer systems.

It's not conspiracy.
It's simply a game you were never invited to learn.

The Moment Everything Changes

Once you see it, you can't unsee it.

- You stop believing that hard work will set you free.

- You stop thinking that following the rules will reward you.

- You stop expecting the system to serve your interests.

Instead, you start asking new questions:

- **How do I control assets?**

- **How do I structure income differently?**

- **How do I multiply money using systems?**

- **How do I legally protect what I build?**

- **How do I escape dependence completely?**

This is where the real game begins.

The journey isn't about shortcuts or get-rich schemes.
It's about learning the forbidden codes you were never supposed to see —
and applying them with discipline.

Most people will never take this step.
They'll stay on the treadmill, endlessly hoping the system changes.

But you don't have to.

In the chapters ahead, you'll be shown the exact codes the elites quietly
use to multiply wealth, protect assets, and exit the trap.

The game you were programmed to lose can now be played to win.

Chapter 2: How the System Keeps You Poor

The Debt-Slavery Model

Most people believe debt is a personal failure.

If you're in debt, it's your fault.
You spent too much.
You mismanaged your money.
You weren't responsible.

That's what the system wants you to believe — that your financial struggle is a personal problem.

In reality, debt is the system's most powerful weapon.
It was engineered to keep you trapped.

Debt Was Never About Helping You

Debt is sold as opportunity:

- A student loan to build your future.

- A mortgage to build your family.

- A car loan to stay mobile.

- A credit card for convenience.

But behind every loan is the same quiet truth:

Every dollar you owe makes you more dependent.

The moment you sign that loan agreement, your freedom shrinks:

- You take jobs you don't want — because bills must be paid.

- You stay at companies that don't serve you — because quitting feels dangerous.

- You sacrifice dreams — because obligations come first.

Debt transforms free people into obedient workers.

The more you owe, the fewer choices you have.

The System Profits While You Struggle

The modern economy is built on your debt.

- Banks profit from your interest.

- Governments profit from your taxes.

- Corporations profit from your consumption.

- Schools profit from your student loans.

The deeper you go into debt, the more valuable you become — not as a free individual, but as a controlled financial unit generating revenue for the system.

Your debt is someone else's asset.

The wealthy don't fear your debt — they profit from it.

The Myth of "Good Debt" vs "Bad Debt" (For the Masses)

You've probably heard:

"Not all debt is bad. There's good debt and bad debt."

The system sells this distinction to justify endless borrowing:

- Good debt: mortgages, student loans, business loans.

- Bad debt: credit cards, personal loans, consumer spending.

But this is only half the truth — and it keeps you trapped.

For the masses:

- "Good debt" still means years of payments.

- "Good debt" still locks you into employment.

- "Good debt" still drains wealth through interest and fees.

For the wealthy:

- Debt becomes leverage.

- Debt funds assets that generate cash flow.

- Debt multiplies wealth while others repay it.

The true game isn't about avoiding debt — it's about controlling it.

Why The System Needs You In Debt

A population drowning in debt:

- Can't easily quit jobs.

- Can't easily protest.

- Can't easily challenge authority.

- Can't easily take risks to build wealth.

They're too busy surviving.

A deeply indebted population is the most controllable population.

Governments quietly encourage borrowing, because debt-fueled growth allows them to expand spending, inflate currency, and maintain political control — while blaming personal responsibility for the fallout.

The more you owe, the more compliant you become.

The First Step to Freedom: See Debt for What It Is

The awakening begins by seeing debt not as an accident, but as a weapon.

It's not about feeling guilty for borrowing.
It's not about blaming yourself for following the script.

It's about realizing the game was designed to pull you in from the start.

- The banks profit whether you succeed or not.

- The system profits whether you work or not.

- The lenders profit whether you struggle or not.

The chains were always invisible — until now.

In the coming chapters, you'll learn how the wealthy use debt differently — as a tool to multiply wealth instead of a chain that limits it.

Because the real game isn't about debt avoidance.
It's about debt mastery.

Taxes: The Legalized Extraction Machine

You were taught that paying taxes is your duty.
That it's fair.
That everyone contributes their share.

That's the story the system sells you.

But the truth is far more brutal:

Taxes are not about fairness — they are the most efficient extraction tool ever created to keep wealth concentrated at the top.

The Highest Taxed Class: You

The system is designed to tax workers the most.

- If you work for a paycheck (W2 income), your taxes are taken before you even touch your money.

- The more you earn through labor, the higher your tax bracket.

- You have little to no access to deductions, credits, or legal shelters.

This is how most people stay trapped:

- You work harder → you make more → you move into a higher tax bracket → you keep less.

- The reward for your effort is not freedom — it's higher extraction.

The harder you work for wages, the more the system takes.

Meanwhile, the wealthy structure income in ways that are barely taxed — or not taxed at all.

How The Wealthy Legally Avoid Taxes

The rich don't evade taxes.
They avoid them — legally — by playing an entirely different game:

- They structure income through businesses and corporations.

- They invest in assets that generate cash flow with preferential tax treatment.

- They use trusts, entities, and legal structures to control income flows.

- They leverage depreciation, cost segregation, and capital gains advantages.

- They borrow against assets to access cash without triggering taxable events.

The tax code rewards those who own — not those who labor.

Why You Were Never Taught This

Because your taxes fund the system that keeps you dependent.

Governments need obedient workers:

- Workers generate tax revenue.

- Workers fuel consumption.

- Workers fund debt-based growth.

- Workers depend on government programs.

The education system never taught you wealth preservation, tax strategy, or legal asset protection — because keeping you financially naive serves the system's interests.

Ignorance keeps you paying.
Knowledge allows you to protect.

The Real Reason Taxes Exist

Publicly, taxes are about funding infrastructure, education, and public services.

Privately, taxes are about control:

- Tax codes are written by those who understand them best — the elites.

- Complex rules create loopholes for insiders.

- Simplicity applies only to the masses — "work, get paid, get taxed."

And as inflation rises, governments collect even more tax revenue while your purchasing power collapses.

The system profits whether you rise or struggle — because the extraction mechanism is built into your labor.

The Awakening

This isn't about tax evasion.
It's about understanding that:

- You've been trained to participate in the most heavily taxed form of income: wages.

- The system incentivizes ownership because ownership creates jobs, stimulates economies, and funds political power.

The game rewards those who step into control — and quietly drains those who remain dependent.

In the chapters ahead, you'll learn how the wealthy legally build structures to shield wealth from taxes — not through illegal schemes, but by using the exact rules that were always available, but never taught.

The extraction machine was designed to be invisible.

Now you see it.

Inflation: How Your Money Is Silently Stolen

Most people feel it long before they can explain it:

- Prices keep rising.

- Bills keep growing.

- Paychecks stretch thinner every year.

They work harder, save more, and yet… they fall behind.

The system tells you this is just "the economy."
In truth, it's one of the most effective wealth extraction tools ever created: inflation.

The Illusion of Rising Costs

You're told that rising prices are natural.

- Gas goes up.

- Food gets more expensive.

- Housing costs explode.

- Education skyrockets.

But while your paycheck inches up slowly, prices sprint ahead.

What you can buy with your money shrinks year after year — silently stealing wealth you've already earned.

This isn't random.
It's engineered.

How Inflation Actually Works

At its core, inflation is simple:

- Governments print more currency.

- More currency chases the same goods and services.

- Prices rise to reflect the diluted value of each dollar.

When governments increase the money supply, every existing dollar loses purchasing power.

Your savings, your wages, your retirement — all quietly eroded.

You worked for those dollars — and the system devalues them after you've earned them.

Who Inflation Truly Serves

Contrary to what you're told, inflation benefits those who control assets and debt.

- The wealthy own assets (real estate, businesses, stocks) that often rise with inflation.
- The wealthy hold debt — which gets cheaper to repay as currency weakens.
- Governments reduce the real value of their debt obligations through inflation.

Meanwhile, wage earners:

- Earn fixed incomes that struggle to keep up.
- Watch savings accounts lose value.
- Pay higher prices for basic necessities.

Inflation quietly transfers wealth from workers to asset holders — from savers to borrowers — from the masses to the elite.

Why Inflation Is The Perfect Weapon

Inflation is invisible.

- You don't see your money being taken.
- You see prices rising — but not why.

- You blame external factors: companies, shortages, bad luck.

This allows politicians, central banks, and corporations to avoid responsibility while quietly expanding their own wealth and control.

You can resist taxes.
You can avoid debt.
But inflation steals from everyone — automatically.

The Programming That Keeps You Blind

The system teaches you:

- Save in cash.

- Work harder for raises.

- Trust the currency.

But in an inflationary system, cash is a dying asset.
The more you save, the more you lose.

The wealthy play the opposite game:

- They store wealth in assets that outpace inflation.

- They borrow cheap money to acquire appreciating assets.

- They allow inflation to erode their debt while growing their wealth.

The rich don't fear inflation — they weaponize it.

The Awakening

The reason you feel like you're running uphill is because you are.

The game was designed that way.

- Work hard.

- Save money.

- Watch your purchasing power shrink.

The system steals most efficiently when you don't even realize you're being robbed.

Once you understand how inflation works, you stop playing defense.

You stop saving in dying currency.
You start acquiring assets.
You start leveraging the very forces designed to trap others.

In the next chapters, we move beyond exposure — and into the forbidden codes that allow you to play the real game.

Chapter 3: Scarcity Programming

How Scarcity Was Programmed Into You

Before the system controlled your money — it controlled your mind.

Wealth doesn't only exist in numbers or assets.
It exists first as **belief systems.**

If you believe that money is scarce, that wealth is dangerous, that success is for "other people" — you will unconsciously sabotage any opportunity that threatens those beliefs.

And that's exactly how the system keeps billions trapped.

You weren't just born into financial slavery — you were programmed to accept it.

The Myth of Limited Wealth

From childhood, you were told:

- Money doesn't grow on trees.

- Rich people are greedy.

- Be thankful for what you have.

- Wanting more is selfish.

- Security is more important than freedom.

- Play it safe. Don't take risks.

These statements sound innocent — even virtuous.
But beneath them is a carefully engineered message:

There isn't enough.
You should settle.
Someone else controls the opportunity.

The Scarcity Cycle

Scarcity isn't just a feeling — it's a self-reinforcing cycle:

- You fear losing what little you have.

- That fear stops you from taking bold action.

- Playing small limits your growth.

- Limited growth reinforces scarcity.

- The system profits from your caution.

The safest path becomes the most expensive trap.

The result?

- You avoid starting businesses.

- You fear investing.

- You stay employed at jobs you hate.

- You view debt as dangerous rather than strategic.

- You obsess over saving pennies while ignoring opportunities to multiply wealth.

Scarcity thinking quietly bleeds your power — before you ever touch a dollar.

Why Scarcity Is Taught (By Design)

Scarcity thinking keeps you easy to control:

- You'll obey authority in exchange for perceived security.

- You won't challenge the system — because you fear losing stability.

- You won't take risks that threaten the power structure.

The system doesn't need to enslave you physically if it can enslave you mentally.

Scarcity programming ensures:

- You stay dependent.

- You don't build ownership.

- You don't accumulate power.

It's easier to manage a population that fears loss than one that builds sovereignty.

The Truth They Don't Teach

Wealth is not scarce.
Money is printed by the trillions.
Assets are created constantly.
New industries emerge every year.

The wealthy aren't lucky — they simply learned to play offense inside an abundant system you were trained to see as limited.

Once you see through the scarcity illusion, the game shifts entirely:

- You stop fearing opportunity.

- You start building ownership.

- You focus on leverage, not labor.

- You seek control, not comfort.

The Awakening

The hardest prison to escape is the one you don't realize you're inside.

Scarcity isn't your nature — it was installed.

And once you uninstall it, wealth becomes a system — not a dream.

In the next chapters, we'll dismantle the guilt and fear you've carried — and replace it with the actual codes used by the wealthy to multiply, protect, and control wealth across generations.

The scarcity program is breaking.
The real codes are waiting.

The Guilt Complex: Why You Fear Wealth

Even when people desire wealth, many secretly feel uncomfortable pursuing it.

They hesitate.
They sabotage opportunities.
They shrink their ambitions.

Why?

Because the system not only teaches you to fear poverty — it teaches you to feel guilty about wealth.

The Morality Trap

From a young age, you were bombarded with messages:

- "Money changes people."

- "Rich people are greedy."

- "It's easier for a camel to pass through the eye of a needle than for a rich man to enter heaven."

- "The pursuit of wealth is selfish."

- "Be grateful for what you have."

These phrases sound righteous.
But behind them lies a subtle form of control:

If you associate wealth with greed, corruption, or evil — you'll naturally avoid building it.

You don't resist wealth because it's bad — you resist it because you've been trained to believe it makes you bad.

Why Guilt is Powerful for Control

A person who feels guilty about pursuing wealth:

- Stays small.

- Avoids ambition.

- Self-sabotages success.

- Accepts mediocrity as virtue.

This benefits the system:

- You remain a worker.

- You serve those who own.

- You don't challenge power structures.

- You become easier to govern, tax, and manage.

A guilty population polices itself.
The system never needs to intervene.

The False Morality of Poverty

The system glorifies struggle:

- The "hardworking poor" are noble.

- The rich are portrayed as villains.

- Sacrifice is seen as virtue.

- Comfort is viewed as selfish.

But poverty does not create virtue.
Struggle does not create wisdom.
Lack does not create morality.

Wealth does not make you evil — it makes you powerful.
Power can be used for good or evil — but poverty rarely empowers anyone.

The wealthy aren't immoral because they have money — many elites are corrupt because they crave control, not because they simply possess wealth.

The Truth the System Hides

Wealth is simply energy and leverage:

- It amplifies who you already are.

- It allows you to create, contribute, and protect.

- It gives you autonomy to live on your terms.

The guilt you feel was implanted to keep you harmless:

- Harmless to governments.

- Harmless to corporations.

- Harmless to power structures.

Because wealth in your hands threatens the dependency they profit from.

If you don't pursue wealth, you remain dependent.
If you feel guilty for building wealth, you'll stay obedient.

The Awakening

The removal of guilt is the gateway to freedom.

You are not bad for wanting wealth.
You are not greedy for seeking ownership.
You are not selfish for refusing financial slavery.

You've simply awakened to a system that trained you to remain small.

In the chapters ahead, we'll dismantle the final psychological chains —
and move into the practical forbidden codes that allow you to build wealth
without permission.

Because guilt was never your burden — it was their tool.

Rewriting Your Internal Codes

The wealth you're capable of building isn't waiting for permission. It's waiting for you to delete the programming that's been controlling you.

Because no amount of strategy can override a mind that secretly believes it's not allowed to win.

You've seen how scarcity and guilt were installed.

Now it's time to install something new.

Rule #1 — Wealth Is Created, Not Distributed

You've been taught that wealth is a limited pie — that for one person to have more, someone else must have less.

This is a lie.

- New businesses are born every day.

- New markets open every year.

- New technologies create new opportunities.

- Money flows constantly between industries, countries, and systems.

Wealth isn't stolen — it's created by those who build, produce, and control value.

The elites don't fear scarcity because they know how to build systems that generate wealth — endlessly.

You must adopt the same builder's mindset:

- You're not taking from others.

- You're not depriving anyone.

- You are building value and systems that generate wealth.

Rule #2 — Ownership Equals Freedom

The core reason most people stay poor is simple:

They own nothing.

- No businesses.

- No real estate.

- No intellectual property.

- No systems that produce income without their labor.

Without ownership, you will always rent your life from someone else.

The rich buy control.
The poor rent security.

Every dollar you make should be seen as fuel for ownership:

- Acquiring assets.

- Building systems.

- Buying time.

- Creating leverage.

Your labor funds your escape — not your consumption.

Rule #3 — Permission Is an Illusion

The system trained you to ask:

- "Is this allowed?"

- "Is this safe?"

- "Am I qualified?"

- "Do I deserve this?"

These questions keep you paralyzed.

The elite never wait for permission — they build structures, acquire leverage, and control outcomes.

The truth is simple:

- The tax code is available to you.

- The legal entities are available to you.

- The credit systems are available to you.

- The asset classes are available to you.

You've simply never been taught how to use them.

The forbidden codes aren't hidden behind locked doors — they're hidden behind your programming.

The Internal Shift

This isn't about empty positivity or fake affirmations.

This is about cold, clear truth:

- You were programmed to fear wealth.

- That program kept you small.

- You can delete it — permanently.

From this point forward:

- You seek ownership, not wages.

- You seek leverage, not labor.

- You seek control, not security.

- You build systems, not just income.

The game begins the moment you take control of your internal codes.

In the next chapters, we move into the forbidden financial codes themselves — the strategies, structures, and systems the elite have quietly mastered for generations.

Scarcity dies now.
Control begins now.

Chapter 4: The Hidden Rules of the 1%

The Knowledge Passed Quietly Between Generations

The greatest advantage the wealthy have isn't just money.
It's access to knowledge that most people never even realize exists.

Because true wealth is not only accumulated — it is taught, transferred, and protected.

While the masses are programmed to start from zero every generation, the 1% operate inside a private system of wealth transmission.

This isn't luck.
It's design.

The Public Curriculum vs The Private Curriculum

The masses are educated with:

- How to be good employees.

- How to save for retirement.

- How to avoid debt.

- How to budget.

- How to work for someone else.

The wealthy are taught privately:

- How to structure assets.

- How to legally avoid taxes.

- How to control wealth through entities and trusts.

- How to multiply capital using debt and leverage.

- How to build systems that generate cash flow across generations.

The most valuable financial knowledge isn't taught in schools — it's passed quietly at dinner tables, in private meetings, and behind closed doors.

The Family Wealth Engine

Generational wealth isn't accidental.
It's engineered.

The wealthy build family-level wealth engines:

- **Trusts** to shield assets from taxes and lawsuits.

- **Family LLCs** to consolidate control and manage wealth as a business.

- **Private banking** to self-fund investments and avoid traditional lenders.

- **Legal tax structures** that minimize extraction.

- **Estate planning** to prevent wealth erosion at death.

- **Education** to teach children how to maintain, grow, and protect assets.

The next generation doesn't start over — they start ahead, fully trained and fully armed.

Why The Masses Never Receive This Knowledge

Because the system is designed for turnover, not preservation.

- The masses work → consume → retire → pass debt to the next generation.

- The system profits from constant resets — each generation starting from zero.

The 1% avoid this cycle entirely.

The true secret isn't just earning wealth — it's creating structures that prevent wealth from leaking.

The education system has no incentive to teach you this.
Politicians have no incentive to expose it.
Financial institutions profit from keeping you financially uneducated.

The wealth codes stay locked inside private networks — while the public fights over wages, inflation, and survival.

The Awakening

The most dangerous lie you were told is that "knowledge is equally available to everyone."

Technically, yes.
In reality, no.

- The information exists — but you were never shown where to find it.

- The structures exist — but you were never taught how to use them.

- The systems exist — but you were programmed to fear them.

The 1% are not special — they were simply trained early, privately, and intentionally.

Now, you enter that private conversation.

In the next sections, we'll begin decoding the exact forbidden structures the elites use to protect, multiply, and quietly transfer wealth — not just for themselves, but for generations that haven't even been born yet.

The wealth engine you were never invited into is about to be exposed.

Private Education vs Public Indoctrination

You were told that education was your path to success.
That school would prepare you for the real world.
That credentials would unlock opportunity.

What you were never told is this:

The system's education was never designed to create wealth-builders — it was designed to create obedient workers.

The Purpose of Public Education

Look at what you were taught:

- Memorize facts.

- Follow instructions.

- Obey authority.

- Pass standardized tests.

- Seek stable employment.

You weren't trained to:

- Build systems.

- Acquire assets.

- Leverage debt.

- Minimize taxes.

- Protect wealth.

- Build autonomy.

The public education system was built to feed the machine — not to free you from it.

It produces employees, not owners.
Dependents, not sovereigns.

The Private Curriculum of the Elite

While you were memorizing state-approved textbooks, the wealthy were learning something very different behind closed doors:

- How to legally structure trusts and entities.

- How to shield assets from lawsuits and taxes.

- How to acquire income-producing assets.

- How to build private banking systems.

- How to borrow money strategically to multiply wealth.

- How to transfer wealth efficiently across generations.

The rules you were playing by were designed for you.
The rules they were playing by were designed for them.

Why This Knowledge Stays Hidden

Because the financial system needs turnover:

- New workers to replace retirees.

- New borrowers to fuel debt markets.

- New consumers to drive corporate profits.

- New taxpayers to fund government expansion.

An obedient, financially naive population is the fuel that keeps the system alive.

If everyone knew how to build wealth structurally:

- The labor supply would shrink.

- Tax revenues would fall.

- Banks would lose borrowers.

- Corporations would lose obedient employees.

The elite don't hide this knowledge by force — they hide it through omission.

They simply never teach you what they teach their own children.

The Financial Silence

Have you ever wondered:

- Why schools don't teach real-world financial systems?

- Why no one explains how the tax code actually works?

- Why credit, debt leverage, and asset protection aren't core subjects?

Because your ignorance is profitable.

When you remain financially untrained:

- You borrow instead of build.

- You consume instead of create.

- You serve instead of own.

You play a game you never designed — while believing you're free.

The Awakening

The most dangerous education isn't the one you received — it's the one you were denied.

You were given enough knowledge to function inside the system — but never enough to escape it.

That changes now.

In the next sections, we'll break down the exact financial structures, tools, and codes the wealthy use to dominate the game — and how you can begin applying them, no matter where you're starting from.

The forbidden curriculum is open.
The real training begins now.

The Mindset of Permanent Control

The biggest difference between the elite and the masses isn't just money.

It's how they think.

The 1% don't think in terms of income — they think in terms of control.

While most people chase paychecks, promotions, and job titles, the wealthy focus on one thing:

Who controls the system that produces the money?

Income vs Infrastructure

Most people are trained to pursue:

- Higher salaries.

- Better benefits.

- Bigger bonuses.

- Retirement packages.

The problem?
None of it creates ownership.

- Salaries stop when you stop working.

- Bonuses depend on someone else's permission.

- Retirement accounts are tied to market risk and inflation.

You own nothing — you rent your entire financial existence.

The wealthy avoid this trap entirely.

They focus on:

- Building systems that generate revenue 24/7.

- Owning assets that appreciate over time.

- Controlling entities that limit personal liability.

- Acquiring cash flow streams that don't require their labor.

They don't chase higher income — they control infrastructure.

Control Is Freedom

Control means:

- Deciding how your wealth is structured.

- Deciding how much you pay in taxes.

- Deciding who has legal access to your assets.

- Deciding how your wealth moves across generations.

- Deciding when and how you work — or if you work at all.

True freedom isn't about how much you make — it's about how much you control.

Without control, even high earners remain vulnerable:

- One lost job.

- One legal issue.

- One health crisis.

- One market crash.

When you don't control the system — you can lose everything overnight.

The Compounding Advantage of Control

Once the wealthy acquire control, they multiply it:

- Tax-advantaged growth compounds faster.

- Asset-protected wealth survives legal attacks.

- Cash flow funds further investments.

- Leverage amplifies returns without risking personal collapse.

- Private education ensures the next generation keeps expanding the empire.

Control compounds — while labor simply exhausts.

The result?

Each generation starts further ahead — because they control more of the game with each cycle.

Why Control Feels Dangerous to the Masses

You've been programmed to believe:

- Ownership is risky.

- Entrepreneurship is unsafe.

- Complexity is for experts.

- Financial structures are for the rich.

The system sold you simplicity — because complexity creates power.

Control feels scary when you've only ever experienced dependence.

That fear keeps most people locked inside systems they don't own — trading freedom for perceived safety.

The Awakening

You were never meant to stay dependent.
You were programmed to remain dependent.

Control isn't reserved for the elite — they simply accessed it first.

Now, you enter that space.

In the next chapters, we begin breaking down the forbidden financial codes that create true control:

- How to legally structure wealth.

- How to shield assets.

- How to multiply money using systems.

- How to exit dependency permanently.

Control isn't given.
It's built.
And your construction begins now.

PART II — THE BLACKLIST

Chapter 5: Forbidden Financial Codes

The True Laws of Wealth Nobody Teaches

You've been shown fragments your whole life.

- Budget your expenses.

- Work harder.

- Save consistently.

- Retire late.

But these are not wealth-building laws.
They are survival rules — designed for those who were never meant to rise.

True wealth follows entirely different laws — laws you were never taught.

Now you'll see them.

Law #1 — Wealth Flows to Ownership, Not Labor

Labor produces income.
Ownership produces wealth.

- The worker earns wages.

- The owner earns profits, dividends, rents, royalties, and capital gains.

Income stops when labor stops.
Ownership compounds whether you work or not.

The wealthy understand that every dollar earned through labor must be redirected into ownership as fast as possible.

- Businesses.

- Intellectual property.

- Real estate.

- Investments.

- Systems that produce income while they sleep.

Labor is the starting fuel.
Ownership is the wealth engine.

Law #2 — Money Is a Tool, Not a Goal

Most people chase money emotionally:

- Fear of not having enough.

- Guilt for wanting more.

- Desire for comfort.

The wealthy view money coldly — as a tool:

- To acquire assets.

- To gain control.

- To create leverage.

- To protect against threats.

- To expand autonomy.

They don't hoard money — they deploy it.

Cash sitting idle loses value to inflation.
Capital deployed into assets compounds exponentially.

Money isn't wealth — systems are.

Law #3 — Debt Multiplies Wealth When Controlled

The masses fear debt.
The elite weaponize it.

- They borrow to acquire appreciating assets.

- They borrow against assets to access tax-free liquidity.

- They use business credit to expand operations without personal liability.

- They leverage other people's money to scale wealth far beyond their personal capital.

Debt becomes dangerous when it funds consumption.
Debt becomes powerful when it funds production.

The wealthy master debt as a tool — while the masses drown in it as a trap.

Law #4 — Taxes Are Negotiated Through Structure

The masses believe taxes are fixed.

- Income tax brackets.

- Payroll taxes.

- Capital gains taxes.

The wealthy understand that taxes are not just rates — they are outcomes of structure.

- LLCs, S-Corps, Trusts.

- Strategic entity stacking.

- Income reclassification.

- Depreciation.

- Cost segregation.

- International strategies.

The tax code is not a punishment — it's a guidebook for the informed.

The more you understand structure, the less you pay — legally.

Law #5 — Stealth Is Power

The masses chase status.
The elite value invisibility.

- Quiet asset accumulation.

- Private trusts.

- Anonymous entities.

- Low public exposure.

- Strategic privacy.

The less the system sees, the harder you are to target.

Stealth wealth protects not only assets — it protects control.

The more visible you are, the more vulnerable you become.

The Awakening

These are the laws you were never shown.

- Not because they're illegal.

- Not because they're inaccessible.

- But because they give you control — and control threatens the system's stability.

You were programmed to believe wealth is complicated, dangerous, or reserved for others.
It never was.

In the next sections, we'll break down these laws into actionable codes you can apply — no matter where you're starting from.

The forbidden knowledge isn't forbidden because it's secret.
It's forbidden because it creates power.
And now it's yours.

The Financial Illusions Sold to the Masses

The most dangerous lie isn't total ignorance — it's false knowledge.

The system doesn't just keep people financially blind — it gives them just enough information to make them believe they're in control.

This illusion is one of the most powerful tools of financial slavery.

Illusion #1 — "If You Work Hard, You'll Be Rewarded"

- You're sold the dream of meritocracy.

- That hard work alone leads to success.

- That time and effort are all you need.

Reality:

- Labor earns wages.

- Wages are taxed heavily.

- Wages rarely compound.

- Wages stop when labor stops.

The wealthy don't trade time — they build systems.
The harder you work without ownership, the deeper you're trapped.

Illusion #2 — "Saving Will Make You Wealthy"

- You're taught to save a portion of every paycheck.

- You're told to put it in low-interest accounts or retirement funds.

- You're praised for "responsible saving."

Reality:

- Inflation erodes cash constantly.

- Savings accounts barely outpace inflation (if at all).

59

- Compound growth through ownership outpaces savings by orders of magnitude.

Saving is financial defense.
Wealth is built through controlled, leveraged offense.

The wealthy use savings for liquidity — not for wealth creation.

Illusion #3 — "Debt Is Dangerous — Avoid It"

- You're warned to stay debt-free.

- You're told debt equals irresponsibility.

- You're praised for eliminating debt.

Reality:

- Debt used for consumption is destructive.

- Debt used for asset acquisition is powerful.

- The wealthy borrow strategically to acquire cash-flowing assets, then let inflation devalue the debt over time.

The masses fear debt because they were only shown its destructive side.
The wealthy master debt because they understand both sides.

Illusion #4 — "Taxes Are Fixed — Just Pay Your Share"

- You're taught that taxes are inevitable.

- You're told that tax avoidance is unethical.

- You're programmed to feel guilty for seeking tax advantages.

Reality:

- The tax code is filled with legal pathways to minimize tax burdens.

- The elite use entities, trusts, depreciation, and income classification to pay far less — legally.

- The system rewards those who create jobs, own assets, and build infrastructure.

You can't out-earn the tax system through labor — you must structure your wealth intelligently.

Illusion #5 — "Retirement Is The Goal"

- You're sold the dream of working for 40 years.
- You save enough to stop working when you're old.
- You hope inflation doesn't destroy your retirement fund.

Reality:

- Retirement is financial stagnation.
- The wealthy don't retire — they shift into higher forms of control.
- Systems continue producing wealth long after active work ends.

Retirement is a product sold to workers — not to owners.

Why The Illusions Work So Well

- They feel safe.
- They sound responsible.
- They're socially accepted.
- They're promoted by media, schools, and financial institutions.

The system gives you just enough financial education to keep you playing the public game — but never enough to escape it.

The Awakening

The reason most people never build wealth isn't lack of intelligence — it's obedience to illusions.

You've followed the rules you were handed.
You were simply handed the wrong playbook.

Now you hold a different one.

In the next section, we'll unlock the doorway into the forbidden system —
the entry point into true wealth that has always existed just outside your
reach.

The illusion is broken.
The codes await.

The Entry Point Into Hidden Wealth

Most people never even realize they're playing the wrong game.

They grind inside a system designed for dependency — hoping for freedom that never arrives.

But once the illusions collapse, one simple truth becomes impossible to ignore:

The system isn't broken.
It's functioning exactly as it was designed — to keep most people trapped while a small few control everything.

The Real Game Is Access, Not Effort

The 1% don't have superior work ethic.
They have superior access:

- Access to knowledge.

- Access to structures.

- Access to networks.

- Access to legal frameworks.

- Access to financial instruments most people don't even know exist.

It's not that wealth-building tools are unavailable — it's that you were never taught how to access and use them.

Your awakening isn't just about rejecting the old game.
It's about entering the private game that has always existed parallel to the public one.

The Entry Point Is Ownership

The common denominator of every forbidden wealth code is this:

You must own.

- Businesses.

- Entities.

- Assets.

- Intellectual property.

- Systems that operate independently of your labor.

Labor alone was always the bait.
Ownership is the door.

Control of assets — not endless labor — is what separates wealth from struggle.

The sooner you shift from earning income to building ownership structures, the sooner you enter the hidden game.

The Power of Structure Over Effort

The wealthy don't succeed because they "try harder."
They succeed because they:

- Structure income streams for tax efficiency.

- Structure legal entities to separate risk from personal liability.

- Structure wealth vehicles that compound indefinitely.

- Structure asset protection layers that shield what they've built.

Structure, not hustle, creates lasting wealth.

You were programmed to think in linear terms:
Work → Earn → Save → Retire.

The hidden game operates exponentially:
Structure → Multiply → Protect → Transfer.

The Silent Gatekeepers

The reason you never learned any of this isn't because the knowledge doesn't exist.

- It's not classified.

- It's not illegal.

- It's not restricted.

It was simply kept out of your education.

The gate was always there.
You just weren't told how to find the door.

Now you see the entry point clearly.

The Awakening

This book is not about theory.
It's not about positive thinking.
It's not about chasing money.

It's about installing the forbidden wealth codes the elite have quietly mastered — and showing you how to apply them with precision.

In the next chapters, we leave exposure behind — and enter application:

- How to weaponize debt.

- How to control wealth through entities.

- How to shield assets from taxes and lawsuits.

- How to quietly build wealth machines that operate independently of your labor.

The forbidden game begins now.
And you're no longer locked out.

Chapter 6: Debt as a Weapon of Wealth

The Power of Leveraged Debt

You were trained to fear debt.

Debt was painted as:

- Dangerous.

- Irresponsible.

- A trap that ruins lives.

And for most people — it is.

Because the system only showed you **consumption debt** — debt used to finance lifestyles you can't afford, funded by labor you haven't earned yet.

But while you were trained to avoid debt, the wealthy were trained to control it.
They never feared debt — they mastered it.

The Masses Borrow to Consume

This is the debt cycle you were shown:

- Student loans.

- Credit cards.

- Car loans.

- Personal loans.

- Mortgages for personal residences.

This debt funds liabilities — things that cost money, depreciate, and produce no income.

You go into debt to buy things you cannot afford — then work your life repaying debt with taxed labor.

The system profits endlessly:

- Banks collect interest.
- Governments collect taxes.
- Corporations sell you depreciating products.

You fuel everyone else's wealth — while shrinking your own.

The Wealthy Borrow to Acquire

The elite operate under a completely different debt code:

- They borrow money to acquire **income-producing assets**.
- They use debt to control businesses, real estate, and investments.
- They borrow at low rates and earn higher returns, creating positive spreads.
- They allow **inflation to erode the real cost of debt** over time.
- They leverage tax laws to deduct interest, further reducing taxable income.

They don't borrow to consume — they borrow to multiply.

The debt funds assets.
The assets generate cash flow.
The cash flow pays the debt.

The asset pays the loan — not their labor.

The Leverage Formula

Wealthy individuals understand a simple but forbidden formula:

Controlled Debt + Cash-Flowing Assets + Tax Efficiency = Accelerated Wealth

- $500,000 in debt can feel terrifying — if you owe it personally.

- But $500,000 borrowed to acquire an asset generating $60,000/year in income, with tenants paying down the principal, while receiving tax advantages?
  That's controlled power.

The wealthy are never afraid of the amount of debt — only the structure and purpose of it.

The Psychological Advantage

The masses stay trapped because of fear:

- Fear of default.

- Fear of risk.

- Fear of complexity.

The wealthy are trained to:

- Analyze risk objectively.

- Use legal structures to separate personal liability.

- Protect downside with asset insulation.

- Leverage credit intelligently to create positive returns.

Fear keeps you small.
Structure keeps them protected.

Why The System Fears You Learning This

If the masses learned to leverage debt like the wealthy:

- The labor force would shrink.

- The credit markets would shift.

- The tax system would face collapse.

- Dependency would weaken.

Financial independence removes you from the system's control mechanisms.

That's why this knowledge is never part of public education.

The Awakening

Debt isn't good or bad — it's neutral.
It's a weapon.

- In untrained hands, it destroys.

- In trained hands, it builds empires.

You're now entering the level where debt becomes a tool — no longer a threat.

In the next sections, we'll break down exactly:

- How the wealthy structure good vs bad debt.

- How they acquire assets with borrowed money.

- How they protect themselves while leveraging aggressively.

The forbidden codes are no longer theory.
Now we start building.

Good Debt vs Bad Debt (And How the Rich Use Both)

The masses are taught that debt is binary:

- "Debt is bad."

- "Stay out of debt."

- "Pay off all debt as fast as possible."

That's the thinking that keeps most people financially small.

The truth is not about avoiding debt — it's about mastering which debt to use, and how to structure it.

The wealthy don't simply avoid bad debt — they aggressively deploy good debt to multiply wealth at scale.

Bad Debt: The Consumer Trap

Bad debt fuels liabilities — things that drain money instead of producing it.

- Credit card debt to fund consumption.

- Auto loans for depreciating vehicles.

- Personal loans for lifestyle upgrades.

- Student loans for degrees that generate little return.

- Mortgages on personal residences (which cost money monthly and produce no income).

Bad debt forces you to work harder just to service the obligations you voluntarily created.

- You borrow → you owe → you labor to repay.

- The system collects: banks, lenders, corporations, governments.

Bad debt enslaves you to your past decisions.

This is the type of debt the system actively markets to you — because it keeps you dependent.

Good Debt: The Wealth Multiplier

Good debt fuels assets — things that generate income, appreciate, or provide leverage.

- Loans to acquire rental real estate producing positive cash flow.

- Business lines of credit to expand operations generating profits.

- Debt leveraged against appreciating investments (at low interest rates).

- Strategic mortgages on income-producing commercial property.

- Business credit cards used for scaling revenue-generating activities.

Good debt creates cash flow streams that service themselves — while multiplying your equity and asset base.

The wealthy aggressively leverage good debt because:

- The asset pays the debt.

- The tax code allows them to deduct interest.

- Inflation reduces the real cost of the debt over time.

- Their personal labor isn't tied to debt repayment.

How The Rich Use Both — But Never Equally

The wealthy may occasionally carry consumer debt — but they structure their financial system so that **productive debt dwarfs destructive debt.**

- They let personal expenses remain minimal compared to growing asset income.

- They offset personal consumption by stacking income from leveraged assets.

- They calculate every debt decision based on return on capital — not emotional fear.

71

They don't fear debt — they fear stagnation.

The masses are terrified of debt because they've only ever used it destructively.

The wealthy are comfortable with debt because they use it structurally.

The Debt Formula of the 1%

If the debt buys income-producing assets that service themselves, grows in value, and provides tax benefits — it's good debt.

If the debt buys liabilities that generate no income and demand your labor to service — it's bad debt.

That's the line.

Why You Were Never Taught This

The system profits most when:

- You fear debt entirely (and stay small).

- Or you misuse debt entirely (and become dependent).

Both outcomes serve the system.
Neither outcome creates sovereignty.

The financial industry profits either way:

- They collect interest on consumer debt.

- They sell you high-interest products.

- They profit from your fear and mistakes.

You were trained to react emotionally to debt — not to control it strategically.

The Awakening

Debt isn't your enemy.
Ignorance is.

The elites aren't lucky — they're trained.
And you are now stepping into that training.

In the next section, we'll break down exactly how the rich use **The Debt Acceleration Formula** to scale wealth aggressively — while remaining protected.

Debt becomes your weapon — not your weakness.

The Debt Acceleration Formula

The wealthy don't simply "use debt."
They engineer debt systems that multiply wealth exponentially — while protecting themselves from personal exposure.

The masses borrow reactively.
The wealthy borrow strategically.

This is where true financial separation begins.

The Core Formula

At the foundation of every elite wealth machine is a simple formula:

Controlled Debt → Acquired Assets → Positive Cash Flow → Compounding Equity → Tax Advantages → Recycled Leverage → Exponential Growth

Let's break it down:

---

1. Controlled Debt

- Debt is never random.

- Debt is structured, calculated, and fully mapped before being acquired.

- Legal entities (LLCs, S-Corps, Trusts) are used to separate personal risk from business risk.

Rule: Never take on personally guaranteed debt to fund consumption.
Take on strategically structured debt to acquire assets.

---

2. Acquired Assets

- Debt funds the acquisition of **income-producing assets**:
    - Rental real estate.

      o   Businesses.

      o   Income-generating intellectual property.

      o   Revenue-producing investments.

The key:

- The asset itself creates cash flow.

- The cash flow services the debt automatically.

The asset feeds the system — not your labor.

---

3. Positive Cash Flow

The asset must generate:

- Enough income to fully cover debt payments, expenses, and reserves.

- Surplus cash flow that can be reinvested into further growth.

Debt becomes irrelevant when the asset pays for itself.

This removes emotional stress while maintaining full financial control.

---

4. Compounding Equity

As the asset produces income:

- Equity grows through debt paydown.

- Appreciation increases asset value.

- Your ownership position strengthens automatically.

Every payment made on the loan increases your wealth position.

You're not just paying off debt — you're building permanent control over appreciating assets.

---

5. Tax Advantages

The wealthy stack tax benefits at every stage:

- Interest deductions reduce taxable income.

- Depreciation offsets rental income.

- Business expenses are written off.

- Capital gains are deferred or eliminated through advanced tax strategies.

Taxes don't shrink their profits — they amplify them through legal structures.

The tax code is designed to reward those who control assets — not those who trade labor.

---

6. Recycled Leverage

As equity builds:

- The wealthy pull cash out of appreciating assets via refinancing or collateralization.

- That cash is then redeployed into acquiring more assets.

- The process repeats — compounding wealth exponentially.

The same dollar works multiple times inside the system.

This is how small amounts of capital, properly leveraged, can scale into multi-million dollar wealth machines.

---

7. Exponential Growth

Each layer feeds the next:

- Controlled debt fuels acquisition.

- Acquisition fuels cash flow.

- Cash flow fuels equity.

- Equity fuels more leverage.

- Leverage fuels further acquisition.

This cycle compounds faster than labor can ever produce.

The wealthy don't work harder year after year — their systems work harder year after year.

Why The Masses Never Use This Formula

- Fear of debt.

- Lack of financial education.

- No exposure to legal structures.

- Emotional attachment to income rather than ownership.

- Dependence on employment as their only security.

The system trained you to avoid the very tools that create financial freedom.

The Awakening

This is the point where the game fully shifts.

You're no longer playing defense.
You're building systems of perpetual motion — wealth engines that compound, protect, and scale independently of your labor.

**You've crossed from income earning into wealth building.
From survival into control.**

In the next chapters, we'll move into the structural side of this system — the legal entities, trusts, and protections the wealthy use to safely operate these powerful debt acceleration machines.

**The game isn't risky — when you know how to build the structure.
Now you will.**

Chapter 7: The Power of Entities

Legal Protection Through Structures

The masses focus on:

- Income.

- Paychecks.

- Savings accounts.

- Personal credit.

The wealthy focus on:

- **Structures.**

Because real power isn't found in how much you make — it's found in how your wealth is legally structured.

Entities aren't just for "big businesses."
They are the legal infrastructure that allows the wealthy to:

- Multiply wealth.

- Protect assets.

- Control tax exposure.

- Shield themselves from personal liability.

You were never taught this — because once you understand entities, you no longer depend on the system's public rules.

The Purpose of Entities

An entity is simply a legal structure that separates you from your assets:

- LLC (Limited Liability Company)

- Corporation (S-Corp, C-Corp)

- Trust (Revocable, Irrevocable, Asset Protection Trusts)

- Partnerships
- Holding Companies

The entity becomes the owner — you control the entity.

This separation is where protection begins.

Legal Separation = Control Without Exposure

Without entities:

- You own assets personally.
- You carry full personal liability.
- Lawsuits, debts, and judgments can directly target your personal wealth.

With entities:

- The entity owns the assets.
- Your personal liability is shielded.
- Creditors, lawsuits, and legal threats hit the entity — not your personal wealth.

The more you own directly, the more vulnerable you are.
The more you own indirectly (through structures), the more protected you become.

The Layers of Protection

The wealthy rarely operate with a single entity.

They stack layers:

- Holding companies own operating companies.
- Operating companies separate different lines of business.
- Trusts hold equity in entities to protect assets from future claims.

- Real estate is held in separate LLCs per property to isolate risk.

Every layer increases protection, control, and flexibility.

The result:

- A lawsuit can attack one property — not your entire empire.

- A business failure doesn't expose your personal residence.

- A creditor can't penetrate properly layered trusts and entities.

The Tax Advantages

Entities aren't just about protection — they're about optimization.

- Business entities allow tax deductions unavailable to individuals.

- Income can be reclassified and taxed more favorably.

- Expenses can be legally deducted against income.

- Entity stacking allows for advanced tax strategies that reduce taxable exposure dramatically.

The tax code rewards structure — not labor.

The masses pay taxes first and live on what's left.
The wealthy structure expenses first and pay tax on what remains.

The System Never Taught You This

Because:

- Schools don't teach entity structures.

- Employers don't benefit from you owning entities.

- Governments prefer W-2 employees who can't deduct or structure.

- Banks profit more from lending to unprotected individuals.

The less you structure, the more you feed the system.

The Awakening

Entities aren't complex — they were simply never explained to you.

- You don't need millions to start.

- You don't need advanced legal degrees.

- You need to understand how to separate ownership from control.

Control everything. Own nothing personally.

This is how the wealthy quietly operate entire empires while remaining legally insulated.

In the next sections, we'll break down exactly which entities the elites use, how they combine them, and how you can start building your own legal fortress — no matter where you're starting from.

The protection phase begins now.

LLCs, Trusts, and Asset Separation

The real power of entities isn't in having "a company."
It's in knowing **how to separate assets, risks, and control across multiple legal layers.**

The wealthy never expose everything to a single point of failure.

This is how they stay untouchable — even when lawsuits, creditors, or crises hit.

✓ LLC: The Wealth Builder's Foundation

Limited Liability Companies (LLCs) are the entry point for most wealth builders.

- **Primary Purpose:** Protect personal assets from business liabilities.

- If the LLC gets sued, your personal house, cars, savings, and other personal assets are shielded.

- LLCs offer pass-through taxation — profits pass directly to owners, avoiding double taxation.

The LLC is your first layer of legal separation.

The wealthy often use multiple LLCs:

- Each property in its own LLC.

- Each business venture in a separate LLC.

- Joint ventures formed with partners using new LLCs.

Rule: The more assets you have, the more you separate them.

✓ Holding Companies: The Second Layer

Wealthy individuals often create **holding companies**:

- An LLC or Corporation that **owns other LLCs.**

- Simplifies management.

- Adds privacy — public records show the holding company as owner, not you directly.

- Creates additional protection by separating ownership from operations.

You don't own the assets — your holding company does.
You control the holding company.

✅ Trusts: The Invisible Fortress

Trusts are the elite's silent power tool.

They allow assets to be:

- **Owned without personal ownership.**

- **Protected from lawsuits, creditors, and divorce.**

- **Transferred generationally without triggering estate taxes.**

Main types used by the wealthy:

- **Revocable Living Trust:**
  - Avoids probate.
  - Simplifies asset transfer upon death.
  - Still within your control while you're alive.

- **Irrevocable Trust:**
  - Removes assets from your personal estate.
  - Offers stronger protection from creditors and lawsuits.
  - Used for advanced estate planning and asset protection.

- **Asset Protection Trusts (APT):**
  - Often offshore or domestic.
  - Shields assets from nearly all legal attacks.

o Complex, but extremely powerful for high-net-worth individuals.

Trusts don't eliminate taxes automatically — they control how assets are exposed and protected across time.

☑ Asset Separation: Never All In One Basket

The wealthy operate under one rule:

Never allow one lawsuit, creditor, or event to collapse your entire system.

- Each asset class lives in separate entities.

- Real estate is divided by property.

- Businesses are segmented into operating and holding entities.

- Personal assets are largely held inside trusts.

- Family wealth is transferred through generational trusts to avoid estate taxes.

Every dollar lives inside multiple legal layers.

☑ The Visibility Advantage

This is how the wealthy remain invisible:

- Their personal name shows little to no asset ownership.

- Public records reflect entities, not individuals.

- Lawsuits see limited recoverable assets.

- Creditors find heavily protected, layered structures.

Privacy is protection.
Structure is power.

✅ Why You Were Never Taught This

- Because the financial system profits from individuals carrying all assets personally.

- Because legal complexity discourages most people from exploring structures.

- Because employers, governments, and financial institutions benefit most when you remain personally exposed.

Financial naivety keeps you profitable — to everyone but yourself.

✅ The Awakening

You don't need to be a billionaire to start structuring like one.

- LLCs can be formed today.

- Holding companies can be created as you scale.

- Trusts can be built as your assets grow.

The longer you wait, the more vulnerable your growing wealth becomes.

In the next section, we'll expose how these structures form an **Invisible Shield** — allowing the wealthy to operate powerfully while staying fully protected.

The wealth fortress continues to build.

The Invisible Shield of the Wealthy

The true power of wealth isn't just in what you own — it's in what you control while appearing to own nothing.

The wealthy build invisible shields that protect their assets, their privacy, and their power — long before any threat appears.

This is how they stay untouchable.

The Visibility Trap

Most people operate fully exposed:

- Their name is attached to every asset.

- Their personal address is on public records.

- Their bank accounts, real estate, vehicles, businesses — all trace directly back to them.

Every asset they own is visible to:

- Lawsuits

- Creditors

- Government agencies

- Predatory attorneys

Visibility is vulnerability.

The system profits when your entire financial life is easily located and targeted.

The Elite Operate in Silence

The wealthy reverse this structure completely:

- Assets are held by entities — not individuals.

- Ownership is fragmented across multiple legal layers.

- Public records show legal entities, not personal names.

- Creditors find nothing personally attached to the individual.

The person owns nothing directly — but controls everything structurally.

This legal distance between you and your assets forms the first layer of the invisible shield.

Layering: The Multi-Shell Structure

The elites don't rely on one entity — they build multiple defensive layers:

- **LLCs hold individual assets.**

- **Holding companies own multiple LLCs.**

- **Trusts own the holding companies.**

- **Foundations sometimes sit above trusts for estate planning.**

The deeper the structure, the harder it becomes for anyone to legally penetrate it.

Even if a lawsuit successfully attacks one entity, the damage is contained — nothing spills into other protected assets.

Control Without Exposure

At the highest levels:

- The wealthy direct entities through power of attorney, managing members, and trustees.

- Their names are often absent from public operating documents.

- Legal structures grant full control — without legal personal exposure.

You don't need to be publicly listed to fully control an empire.

This allows the wealthy to operate confidently — regardless of lawsuits, divorces, economic crashes, or personal crises.

Lawsuit-Proof by Design

Lawsuits thrive on exposed assets:

- Lawyers search public databases for real estate, businesses, and financial accounts.
- The easier your wealth is to locate, the more attractive you become as a legal target.

The wealthy operate invisibly:

- Their homes are owned by trusts or LLCs.
- Their businesses are operated through layered entities.
- Their wealth moves quietly behind legal shields.

Predators can't attack what they can't find.

Why This Knowledge Is Hidden

The masses are never taught:

- Entity layering.
- Asset fragmentation.
- Privacy trusts.
- Corporate veils.

Because:

- Banks, courts, and governments operate more easily when your financial life is exposed.
- The system profits when your assets are vulnerable.
- Lawsuits fund the legal industry — and exposed assets keep that machine running.

The less protection you have, the more valuable you are to others.

The Awakening

Privacy is not secrecy.
Protection is not evasion.
Control is not corruption.

The wealthy simply operate under a legal framework you were never invited to learn.

You can build your own invisible shield — starting with simple entity separation, and expanding as your wealth grows.

The less exposed you are, the stronger you become.
Visibility feeds the system.
Invisibility frees you from it.

Chapter 8: Tax Secrets of the Ultra-Rich

How the Wealthy Legally Minimize Taxes

Most people believe taxes are simple:

- You work.

- You get paid.

- The government takes its share.

End of story.

But for the wealthy, taxes aren't something to fear — they're something to **engineer**.

Because tax law isn't designed to punish wealth — it's designed to reward those who control capital, create jobs, and build infrastructure.

The Two Tax Systems

There are really two tax systems operating side-by-side:

1. The **Public System** — designed for employees, wage earners, and the financially naive.
2. The **Private System** — designed for business owners, investors, and wealth controllers.

You weren't born into the wrong system — you were simply never trained to enter the right one.

Why Wages Are Taxed the Heaviest

W-2 income is:

- The highest taxed form of income.

- Taxed before you receive it.

- Fully exposed to payroll taxes, income taxes, and benefit reductions.

The system extracts maximum value from labor — because labor is easy to tax, track, and control.

The more you work, the more they take.

This is why even high-income earners often remain trapped.

The Wealthy Reclassify Income

The ultra-rich shift income away from wages and into favored categories:

- **Business Income** → taxed at lower rates, with large deductions.
- **Dividends & Capital Gains** → often taxed at far lower rates than earned income.
- **Rental Income** → offset by depreciation.
- **Borrowed Money (Debt)** → not taxable at all.

The key isn't how much you earn — it's how your earnings are classified.

Business Entities As Tax Shields

Entities like LLCs, S-Corps, and Partnerships allow the wealthy to:

- Deduct legitimate business expenses:
    - Travel
    - Vehicles
    - Education
    - Equipment
    - Professional services
- Pay themselves through more favorable structures.
- Control the timing and form of income.

Expenses are deducted first.
Taxes are paid on what's left — not on the gross income.

Depreciation: The Invisible Deduction

One of the most powerful tools:

- Assets like real estate can be depreciated over time.

- Depreciation creates a non-cash expense that reduces taxable income — even while the asset appreciates in real value.

- Entire properties can generate massive paper deductions while still producing positive cash flow.

You collect cash while reporting losses on paper.

Debt: The Untaxed Liquidity Source

- The wealthy borrow against appreciating assets.

- Borrowed funds are not taxable income.

- They access millions in liquidity without triggering taxable events.

You can live tax-free off debt-backed liquidity — while your assets continue to grow untouched.

This is why many billionaires show minimal taxable income while controlling vast empires.

Why You Were Never Taught This

Because:

- Employees generate predictable tax revenue.

- Governments need tax stability.

- The financial system profits when you remain exposed.

- Schools are designed to produce compliant workers — not tax strategists.

You were trained to follow — not to structure.

The Awakening

The ultra-rich aren't breaking laws — they're simply playing a game you were never shown.

The tax code is not your enemy — it's a rulebook.
And you've simply never been taught how to read it.

In the next sections, we'll go even deeper into the specific tax structures and shelters the elite quietly use to protect entire empires across generations.

You don't beat the tax system by avoiding it — you beat it by understanding how it was truly written.

The Tax Code as a Wealth-Building Tool

The masses see taxes as punishment.

The wealthy see taxes as **leverage**.

Because the tax code was never written to crush wealth — it was written to guide capital into places the system wants it to go.

Those who understand this don't just reduce taxes — they use tax law to actively multiply wealth.

The Government Incentive Model

Governments want certain things built:

- Jobs.

- Housing.

- Innovation.

- Infrastructure.

- Economic growth.

But governments can't build these things directly — they rely on private capital to do it.

The tax code is filled with incentives for those who help build what governments need.

The wealthy position themselves where these incentives exist — and are rewarded accordingly.

Tax Shelters That Multiply Wealth

Real Estate: The Tax Shelter King

- Depreciation allows owners to claim tax losses while collecting positive cash flow.

- Cost segregation accelerates depreciation into the early years — maximizing upfront deductions.

- 1031 exchanges allow deferral of capital gains when selling properties and rolling into new ones.

You can scale real estate empires while legally deferring taxes for decades.

Business Ownership: The Expense Shield

- Nearly every legitimate business expense becomes tax-deductible:
    - Travel.
    - Vehicles.
    - Education.
    - Health insurance.
    - Equipment.
    - Retirement plan contributions.

- Income flows through entities, allowing precise control over how much is exposed to taxation.

Owning businesses turns ordinary life expenses into legal tax shields.

Debt & Leverage: The Untaxed Liquidity

- Borrowing against appreciating assets generates tax-free liquidity.

- Lines of credit secured by investments or real estate are not taxable income.

- This borrowed capital funds further asset acquisition — compounding wealth without triggering taxable events.

The wealthiest live off borrowed money while their assets quietly grow.

Charitable Foundations: The Philanthropy Loop

- Private foundations allow the wealthy to:

    o Donate to themselves.

    o Reduce taxable income.

    o Retain control over how funds are distributed.

- Foundations convert taxable income into long-term controlled capital pools.

Charity becomes both a legacy vehicle and a tax management tool.

The Game Inside the Game

- Tax law is not broken — it works exactly as written.

- The wealthy don't exploit loopholes — they follow incentives intentionally written into law.

You're not playing against the system — you're playing inside the rulebook written for those who understand capital.

Why You Were Trained To Ignore This

Because:

- Employees can't access these tools.

- Financial ignorance feeds tax revenue stability.

- Fear of "complicated" tax systems keeps most people passive.

- The wealthy prefer fewer people accessing these same advantages.

Financial literacy is dangerous — to the system.

The Awakening

The tax code is not a prison — it's a blueprint.

- The more you build, the more protection you're granted.

- The more jobs you create, the more credits you earn.

- The more systems you build, the more tax shields you unlock.

The tax system isn't rigged against wealth — it's engineered to reward those who step into control.

In the next section, we'll expose how the ultra-rich **fully shelter income** — creating legal fortresses that make taxable income nearly irrelevant.

The forbidden codes don't avoid taxes — they use taxes to build empires.

Sheltering Income Like the 1%

The true secret isn't just about earning more — it's about keeping more.

The 1% don't just make money differently — they shelter it differently.

Their entire system is designed to minimize what gets exposed to taxation while keeping wealth fully under their control.

The Two Critical Concepts: Exposure vs Control

For the wealthy, income exposure is a choice.
They understand:

- The more income you expose directly, the more you owe.

- The more income you route through structures, the less you expose.

The goal is not to evade — it's to legally reposition income into protected lanes the tax code favors.

The rich control the flow — not the paycheck.

Entity Stacking: Layered Income Streams

The wealthy rarely operate with a single entity:

- LLCs own separate assets.

- Holding companies control multiple LLCs.

- Management companies oversee operations.

- Trusts own the holding and management companies.

- Private foundations manage philanthropy layers.

Each entity serves a purpose:

- Allocating income.

- Redirecting liability.

- Restructuring tax exposure.

- Facilitating generational transfers.

When income hits personal accounts directly, you're taxed like everyone else.
When income flows through structured entities, you control how and when taxation occurs.

Income Splitting: Spreading Exposure

The wealthy rarely concentrate income in one place:

- Different businesses generate income into separate entities.

- Spouses and family members are often made partial owners or employees, distributing income across multiple taxpayers.

- Passive income streams are classified differently than active earned income, taking advantage of favorable rates.

The goal isn't to eliminate income — it's to spread, reclassify, and redirect it across protected vehicles.

This drastically reduces effective tax rates while maintaining full legal compliance.

Deferred Compensation & Retirement Vehicles

While the masses rely on standard retirement accounts, the elite engineer custom plans:

- Defined benefit plans.

- Cash balance pension plans.

- Private deferred compensation agreements.

- Executive bonus structures tied to insurance products.

These allow:

- Delaying taxable income into lower tax years.

- Compounding returns inside tax-sheltered environments.

- Retaining full legal control over large portions of their wealth.

They defer income strategically while their investments grow silently behind legal walls.

Insurance as Tax Shelter

High-net-worth individuals often leverage life insurance policies far beyond simple death benefits:

- Permanent life insurance policies accumulate tax-deferred cash value.

- Policy loans allow tax-free access to that capital during life.

- Upon death, death benefits transfer outside of taxable estates.

Properly engineered, insurance becomes a private tax-free bank the IRS can't touch.

Offshore Entities & Jurisdictional Arbitrage

At higher levels of wealth:

- Offshore trusts and corporations add additional layers of protection.

- International banking offers further privacy and asset protection.

- Jurisdictional arbitrage allows assets to exist outside high-tax, high-litigation zones.

While not necessary for most, these structures exist for those operating in the upper echelons of global wealth protection.

The IRS Still Gets Paid — But Less Than You Think

The ultra-rich pay taxes — but often at fractions of what wage earners pay:

- They control what counts as income.

- They control when income is recognized.

- They control where income is legally located.

- They control how much exposure occurs each year.

The masses work for taxable wages.
The wealthy build tax-optimized systems that pay them
strategically.

Why This Remains Hidden

The average person never learns this because:

- Schools don't teach tax structuring.

- Financial advisors rarely specialize in high-level entity planning.

- The system prefers you stay simple — wages, W-2, standard deductions.

- Complexity discourages investigation.

The simpler your financial life, the easier you are to tax.

The Awakening

You don't need $10 million to start structuring like the 1%.

- LLCs can shield business and real estate income.

- Trusts can begin protecting family assets.

- Strategic compensation plans can reduce taxable exposure.

The tax code isn't reserved for the elite — it's simply mastered by
them.

In the coming chapters, you'll learn how the wealthy **build cash flow engines** that operate entirely outside the 9-5 world, using these exact principles as their financial foundation.

The rules were never hidden.
They were simply never taught.
Now you hold them.

Chapter 9: Credit Alchemy

The True Power of Personal and Business Credit

For most people, credit is a trap.

- Credit cards fund consumption.

- Late payments destroy scores.

- High-interest debt spirals out of control.

But for the wealthy, credit is not danger — it's power.

When mastered, credit becomes one of the most powerful wealth acceleration tools available.

Credit as a Lever, Not a Lifeline

The masses use credit to:

- Buy depreciating assets.

- Fund lifestyles they can't afford.

- Create short-term comfort at long-term cost.

The wealthy use credit to:

- Acquire income-producing assets.

- Scale businesses without risking personal capital.

- Unlock liquidity for wealth multiplication.

- Build relationships with lenders for future leverage.

The purpose is entirely different — consumption vs multiplication.

Personal Credit: The First Gate

Your personal credit profile is your starting point.

- High personal credit scores open doors to business funding.

- Lenders see responsible management, not risky behavior.

- Personal credit unlocks low-interest rates that the wealthy use to fund scalable ventures.

The wealthy maintain:

- High credit limits.

- Low utilization ratios.

- Perfect payment histories.

- Strategic use of credit products designed for rewards and leverage.

Personal credit isn't used to fund lifestyle — it's managed to fuel larger systems.

Business Credit: The Expansion Engine

Once personal credit is optimized, the wealthy shift focus to business credit:

- Business credit is tied to the entity — not personal credit.

- Properly built, business credit grows independently of personal exposure.

- Large lines of credit can fund inventory, operations, marketing, or acquisitions.

Business credit allows you to scale aggressively while preserving personal financial insulation.

Why Business Credit Is So Powerful

- Higher credit limits.

- No personal guarantees after seasoning.

- Business expenses are often tax-deductible.

- Credit utilization doesn't damage personal credit profiles.

The wealthy structure multiple entities, each building its own credit profile, creating massive borrowing capacity across various ventures.

One personal profile. Multiple business credit engines.

The Bank Relationship Code

The ultra-rich know:

- Banks are partners, not obstacles.

- Relationships with private bankers unlock higher funding levels.

- High deposit activity, clean records, and consistent management build lender trust.

Banks lend more easily to those who:

- Already control assets.

- Demonstrate responsible leverage.

- Build trust through structured financial behavior.

Banks reward control — not desperation.

Credit is a Weapon — or a Chain

For the masses:

- Credit funds consumption.

- Consumption fuels debt slavery.

For the wealthy:

- Credit funds assets.

- Assets create income.

- Income repays debt.

- Debt fuels further expansion.

Same tool.
Radically different outcomes.

Why This Is Hidden

- Schools teach nothing about credit leverage.

- Banks profit heavily from irresponsible consumer credit.

- The system benefits when you stay fearful of debt and addicted to consumption.

Controlled ignorance feeds credit profits.
Mastery removes you from the credit trap entirely.

The Awakening

Credit isn't your enemy.
Poor credit behavior is.

Once you master credit:

- Banks become your allies.

- Capital becomes accessible.

- Leverage becomes safe.

- Expansion becomes exponential.

In the next sections, we'll break down how the wealthy build **credit stacking systems** — creating multiple funding streams across entities while maintaining total legal control.

Credit doesn't enslave them — it accelerates them.
And now, it can do the same for you.

Building Multi-Entity Credit Stacking

Most people view credit as a single score attached to their personal identity.

The wealthy view credit as a scalable system — built across multiple entities, with multiple funding lines, all operating simultaneously.

This is credit stacking — one of the most powerful scaling engines available.

One Personal Credit File — Multiple Business Profiles

Your personal credit opens the first door:

- Excellent personal credit allows you to create your first business credit profile.

- Once business credit is established, each entity builds its own separate credit file, independent of your personal score.

The key is entity separation — not everything tied to your personal SSN.

How Credit Stacking Works

1. Establish your first entity (LLC or Corporation).

- Obtain EIN (Employer Identification Number).

- Open a business bank account.

2. Build business credit:

- Start with vendor tradelines (Net 30 accounts).

- Pay all accounts early.

- Add small secured business credit cards.

3. Season the file:

- 3-6 months of perfect payment history builds lender confidence.

4. Apply for unsecured business credit lines:

- Business credit cards.

- Business lines of credit.

- Equipment financing.

5. Repeat the process across multiple entities:

- Each LLC builds its own credit file.

- No personal guarantees required after seasoning.

- Multiple entities = multiple funding streams.

One personal profile becomes the launch pad for several independent funding machines.

Why This Is So Powerful

- Business credit limits grow far faster than personal credit limits.

- Business credit isn't reported to personal bureaus, protecting your personal score.

- Credit stacking creates redundant access to capital across multiple businesses.

The more entities you control, the more credit engines you operate.

How the Wealthy Use Credit Stacking

- Fund real estate acquisitions.

- Scale ecommerce or inventory-based businesses.

- Finance large marketing campaigns.

- Acquire other businesses using credit leverage.

- Build liquidity buffers without personal risk.

This isn't theory — this is how scalable wealth empires are funded quietly.

Risk Isolation Through Entity Separation

Each entity protects:

- The assets inside it.

- The credit tied to it.

- The risk exposure contained within it.

If one business faces challenges:

- Other entities remain fully intact.

- Credit lines remain unaffected across your full stack.

- Personal assets remain legally separated.

The system is designed to survive individual failures without collapsing your entire empire.

The Bank's Perspective

Banks reward:

- Responsible entity management.

- Diversification of credit exposure.

- Clean payment histories.

- Proof of controlled leverage.

The better your structure, the more funding banks offer — because your risk profile looks professionally engineered.

Why This Knowledge Is Hidden

- The system profits when you stay locked into personal consumer credit.

- Most people are never shown business entity leverage.

- Credit stacking takes discipline and knowledge — two things never taught in public education.

Credit stacking removes you from dependency — and dependency is profitable for the system.

The Awakening

You don't need millions to start stacking.

- One LLC.

- One clean personal credit file.

- One disciplined system of management.

And from there, you multiply.

In the next section, we'll break down how the elite protect these stacked systems from collapse — using credit insulation strategies that make their empire nearly bulletproof.

The wealthy don't borrow randomly — they build engineered funding machines.
Now you do too.

Insulating Credit Risk and Protecting the Stack

Building credit stacking systems is only part of the game.

The real power is in building credit structures that are protected — so one failure doesn't collapse your entire system.

This is where the wealthy move from credit growth → to credit resilience.

The Weak Spot Most People Miss

The average borrower:

- Piles all debt under personal credit.

- Personally guarantees everything.

- Ties multiple loans and businesses to a single profile.

- Becomes fully exposed to default risk.

One mistake can destroy their credit and financial future overnight.

The wealthy eliminate these vulnerabilities through **insulation.**

Rule #1 — Minimize Personal Guarantees

- In early stages, personal guarantees may be necessary to open initial business credit lines.

- As business credit profiles season, the goal is full separation.

- The wealthy aggressively negotiate **non-recourse** business loans and lines that do not attach to personal credit.

Your personal credit becomes the launch pad — not the lifelong guarantor.

Rule #2 — Isolate Entities By Function

Each business serves one purpose:

- One LLC for rental real estate.

- Another LLC for consulting income.

- A separate corporation for ecommerce.

- Individual holding companies for ownership consolidation.

One business failure doesn't impact other income streams or credit lines.

If legal, financial, or operational issues strike one entity — the others remain untouched.

Rule #3 — Never Cross-Collateralize

Many banks will offer larger loans if you pledge multiple assets across different entities.

The wealthy avoid this trap.

- Cross-collateralization ties unrelated assets together.

- One default can trigger cascading seizures across multiple properties or businesses.

Keep each asset siloed.
Protect each stream individually.

Rule #4 — Build Liquidity Buffers

The wealthy maintain:

- High cash reserves.

- Business emergency funds.

- Access to untapped lines of credit.

This allows:

- Payment flexibility during market shocks.

- Negotiation leverage with lenders.

- Protection from forced liquidation.

Liquidity prevents small problems from becoming catastrophic failures.

Rule #5 — Insurance as Final Backstop

The elite protect credit stacks with:

- Business liability insurance.
- Key person insurance.
- Umbrella liability policies.
- Property-specific insurance.

This shields cash flow and credit standing when:

- Lawsuits occur.
- Market corrections hit.
- Health crises strike leadership.
- Unexpected losses threaten operations.

Insurance protects both operations and the credit infrastructure built around them.

Rule #6 — Maintain Active Bank Relationships

Strong relationships with:

- Private bankers.
- Business loan officers.
- Commercial lenders.

Banks extend more favorable terms to borrowers who operate like professionals — not desperate credit seekers.

The stronger the relationship, the more flexibility you gain during turbulent seasons.

The Wealth Stack Is Designed for Survival

The wealthy don't just build systems to grow fast — they build systems to **withstand impact.**

- Diversification.

- Entity separation.

- Legal insulation.

- Credit protection.

- Cash flow buffers.

Their wealth stacks aren't fragile — they're engineered for long-term indestructibility.

The Awakening

Credit stacking is not a one-time trick — it's a lifelong strategy.

- You build.

- You insulate.

- You scale.

- You protect.

The longer you operate with this system, the harder you are to stop.

In the next chapters, we move into the final stage — how the wealthy quietly build **private wealth machines** that generate unstoppable cash flow outside the employment system entirely.

You're no longer borrowing reactively.
You're building sovereign funding systems the system cannot control.

Chapter 10: Private Wealth Machines

Building Cash Flow Engines Outside The System

Most people chase income.

- Work harder.

- Get promoted.

- Earn a bigger salary.

But salaries are fragile:

- They stop when you stop working.

- They rise slowly while taxes rise faster.

- They keep you dependent on someone else's permission.

The wealthy don't chase income — they build private wealth machines.

Machines that produce continuous cash flow — with or without personal labor.

The Private Wealth Machine Defined

A **wealth machine** is a system that:

- Acquires assets.

- Produces income.

- Compounds equity.

- Minimizes taxes.

- Insulates risk.

- Scales automatically.

Once built, it operates like a private financial engine — detached from fragile employment systems.

Wealth Machine #1 — Income-Producing Real Estate

The foundation for many wealthy families:

- Rental properties generate monthly cash flow.

- Tenants pay down debt while equity grows.

- Appreciation compounds net worth over time.

- Tax advantages (depreciation, cost segregation, 1031 exchanges) shield income.

Properly structured, real estate becomes a permanent, tax-advantaged income stream.

The wealthy often structure real estate portfolios across multiple LLCs for protection and scalability.

Wealth Machine #2 — Automated Business Systems

The elite don't build businesses that rely on personal labor — they build **systems that operate with or without them.**

- Ecommerce businesses.

- Licensing and royalties.

- Franchises.

- Subscription models.

- Scalable consulting models with delegated fulfillment.

Revenue flows without the owner trading hours for dollars.

Employees, contractors, technology, and automation allow the machine to operate independently.

Wealth Machine #3 — Intellectual Property & Licensing

The wealthy monetize knowledge:

- Books.

- Courses.

- Software.

- Licenses.

- Royalties.

Create once — monetize indefinitely.

These income streams often require little ongoing labor but can generate revenue for years, even decades.

Wealth Machine #4 — Private Lending & Financing

As wealth grows:

- The elite become lenders, not just borrowers.

- Private loans secured by collateral.

- Lending to businesses, real estate projects, or secured notes.

Private lending creates consistent cash flow, high returns, and asset-backed safety.

Instead of borrowing from banks, the wealthy often **become the bank** themselves.

Wealth Machine #5 — Private Investment Vehicles

- Private equity.

- Hedge funds.

- Joint ventures.

- Syndications.

- Angel investing.

These investments:

- Produce passive distributions.

- Provide equity growth.

- Often offer additional tax advantages.

Capital compounds quietly inside private markets inaccessible to the general public.

Why These Machines Work Outside The System

- They don't require employment.

- They operate even in economic downturns.

- They're tax-advantaged by design.

- They scale exponentially with proper structure.

Private wealth machines reduce dependency on any one income source or economic condition.

Why You Were Never Taught This

- Schools teach job security — not wealth independence.

- Governments benefit from steady labor-based tax revenue.

- Corporations profit from your labor dependency.

- Financial institutions profit from your consumer debt.

If you knew how to build private wealth machines, you'd exit the system they profit from.

The Awakening

The wealthy don't work harder — they build systems that work endlessly.

Your goal isn't to replace labor with luck — it's to replace labor with machines.

In the next sections, we'll break down how these machines are stacked together — forming **autonomous wealth engines** that operate across multiple asset classes, protected by layers of legal structures.

You're not chasing income anymore.
You're engineering freedom.

Stacking Income Streams for Financial Autonomy

One income stream is never enough.

The wealthy don't just build one cash flow machine — they stack multiple engines together, creating unstoppable financial ecosystems.

This stacking strategy is what permanently removes them from financial fragility.

The Fragility of Single Income

Most people:

- Depend on one employer.

- Rely on one paycheck.

- Have no insulation if income stops.

One job loss, one economic shock, one health crisis — and everything collapses.

Single income equals maximum risk.

The Wealth Stack: Multiple Independent Streams

The wealthy reverse this:

- Real estate income.

- Business profits.

- Royalties and licensing.

- Private lending.

- Investment distributions.

- Dividend income.

- Interest from lending platforms.

- Private equity payouts.

Each income stream operates independently — failure in one does not collapse the system.

When properly stacked:

- Cash flow becomes reliable.
- Financial stress disappears.
- Growth accelerates.

Layer 1 — Foundation Cash Flow

The first layer covers basic lifestyle expenses:

- Rental income.
- Low-risk business profits.
- Predictable royalty or licensing payments.

This foundation creates peace of mind — financial survival is fully covered.

The wealthy make sure this layer operates with maximum consistency, even during market fluctuations.

Layer 2 — Growth & Scaling

The second layer focuses on:

- Business expansion.
- Higher-yield private investments.
- Growth-focused real estate acquisitions.
- Scalable ecommerce or licensing businesses.

This layer builds wealth beyond survival — expanding net worth and long-term capital.

Surplus cash flow from the foundation layer fuels scaling activities here.

Layer 3 — Long-Term Legacy Capital

The final layer focuses on:

- Trust structures.

- Generational wealth vehicles.

- Asset protection systems.

- Foundations and philanthropic entities.

This layer preserves wealth across decades — shielding it from taxation, lawsuits, and systemic collapse.

The goal is not just personal freedom — it's generational control.

The Power of Redundancy

The stacking model creates:

- Multiple income sources.

- Multiple legal structures.

- Multiple geographic jurisdictions.

- Multiple banking relationships.

- Multiple asset classes.

Redundancy equals resilience.

The wealth machine is no longer vulnerable to:

- Job loss.

- Tax law changes.

- Economic recessions.

- Industry collapse.

- Political shifts.

The Psychological Shift

The wealthy stop asking:

- "How much am I earning this year?"

They ask:

- "How many machines are running?"
- "How many streams are feeding my system?"
- "How many layers protect my wealth?"

They think in terms of systems — not income.

Why This Is Never Taught

- Employees trapped in single income streams are easier to control.
- Single income taxpayers produce steady revenue for governments.
- Fragile financial lives fuel corporate profits through borrowing and consumption.

Stacked wealth equals independence — and independence threatens systemic control.

The Awakening

You don't need extreme wealth to start stacking.

- One rental property.
- One business income stream.
- One licensing or royalty deal.
- One small lending operation.

Each additional stream weakens your dependency.

In the next section, we'll break down **how the wealthy automate these stacks** — building wealth machines that run 24/7 without constant oversight.

We're not just stacking anymore — we're engineering autonomous wealth systems.

Automating Wealth Machines for Perpetual Growth

The wealthy don't just build multiple income streams — they engineer wealth machines that **run without constant personal effort.**

The ultimate freedom isn't high income — it's autonomous income.

Automation transforms stacked wealth into perpetual growth.

Labor Is the Bottleneck

For the masses:

- Income stops when work stops.

- Growth depends on personal energy.

- Time limits scale.

The wealthy eliminate the labor bottleneck by replacing effort with **systems.**

They build machines that grow whether they're present or not.

Rule #1 — Automate Operations

For businesses:

- Outsource daily management to trained staff.

- Delegate operations to contractors or virtual assistants.

- Implement SOPs (Standard Operating Procedures).

- Use software for inventory, payments, customer service, scheduling, and fulfillment.

The business produces income whether the owner works or sleeps.

Rule #2 — Automate Cash Flow Monitoring

The wealthy don't micromanage:

- Banking alerts monitor account balances.

- Automated reports track rent collections, loan payments, and investment returns.

- Accounting software reconciles transactions.

- Tax documents auto-generate from integrated systems.

Automation reduces oversight while maintaining control.

Rule #3 — Automate Capital Deployment

Excess capital doesn't sit idle:

- Auto-invest contributions into brokerage, real estate syndications, or lending platforms.

- Scheduled reinvestments compound returns without manual involvement.

- Automated dividend reinvestment programs (DRIPs) accelerate equity growth.

Capital compounds automatically while remaining fully deployed.

Rule #4 — Automate Risk Mitigation

Wealth machines are protected by:

- Auto-paid insurance policies.

- Asset protection trusts maintaining compliance.

- Scheduled legal reviews to update structures.

- Ongoing credit monitoring and fraud protection services.

The machine defends itself without requiring constant oversight.

Rule #5 — Build Management Teams

High-level wealth owners:

- Hire CFOs, attorneys, CPAs, and wealth managers.

- Outsource oversight to professionals who maintain systems.

- Leverage advisory boards for specialized expertise.

The wealth builder becomes CEO — not operator.

The team maintains, protects, and grows the machine on your behalf.

Rule #6 — Automate Estate Continuity

The wealthy plan beyond themselves:

- Living trusts auto-transfer assets upon death.

- Estate documents update regularly.

- Successor trustees and corporate officers continue operations.

Death doesn't stop wealth machines — the system transitions automatically to heirs.

Why Automation is the Forbidden Key

- Autonomous wealth threatens employer control.

- Governments prefer dependent taxpayers.

- The financial system profits from manual labor income streams.

Fully automated wealth is rarely taught — because it breaks systemic dependency.

The Awakening

You don't automate after reaching extreme wealth — you automate from the start:

- Automate small systems.

- Stack them slowly.

- Expand automation as wealth compounds.

Your labor isn't required forever — only your system-building discipline.

In the next chapter, we'll expose how the ultra-rich **transfer these machines across generations** — ensuring that once wealth is built, it can never be reset to zero.

You're no longer working for wealth.
Your machines are working for you — permanently.

PART III — THE ESCAPE PLAN

Chapter 11: Generational Wealth Engineering

Why Most Family Wealth Disappears — And How the 1% Prevent It

For most families, wealth is temporary.

- The first generation builds it.
- The second enjoys it.
- The third loses it.

This is called "Shirtsleeves to shirtsleeves in three generations."

But the ultra-wealthy break this pattern — by engineering wealth transfer systems that last for centuries.

Why Family Wealth Collapses

1. Lack of Structure:

- Assets are held personally.
- No legal protections are in place.
- Courts, creditors, and taxes strip wealth on transfer.

2. Lack of Education:

- Heirs inherit money without knowledge.
- Poor decisions destroy capital quickly.

3. Emotional Mismanagement:

- Wealth fuels consumption.

- Entitlement replaces stewardship.

- Conflicts erupt among heirs.

Without systems and training, even large fortunes evaporate.

How The Ultra-Rich Break the Cycle

They don't just transfer assets — they transfer control, education, and structure.

Their systems are designed to:

- Preserve capital.

- Maintain privacy.

- Prevent legal battles.

- Train heirs as stewards.

- Legally limit tax exposure.

The Core Pillars of Generational Wealth Preservation

Pillar 1 — Trust Structures

- Irrevocable trusts hold assets.

- Trustees manage distribution rules.

- Courts cannot easily interfere.

- Assets remain protected from divorces, lawsuits, and creditor claims.

Pillar 2 — Family Governance

- Wealth education begins early.

- Heirs are trained in finance, law, and stewardship.

- Family meetings enforce shared vision and discipline.

Pillar 3 — Control Mechanisms

- Spendthrift clauses limit reckless withdrawals.

- Co-trustees ensure responsible decision-making.

- Distributions are tied to behavior, milestones, or merit.

The system protects wealth from both external threats and internal weaknesses.

The Wealth Transfer System

The wealthy engineer:

- **Living Trusts** to avoid probate.

- **Irrevocable Trusts** for asset protection.

- **Family Limited Partnerships (FLPs)** to consolidate control.

- **Dynasty Trusts** that protect wealth for 100+ years.

- **Charitable Foundations** to manage legacy giving.

Each layer creates legal, tax, and control advantages that preserve wealth across generations.

The Estate Tax Defense

- The U.S. estate tax can claim up to 40% of large estates.

- The wealthy avoid this through:
    - Lifetime gifting strategies.
    - Valuation discounts via FLPs.
    - Advanced insurance-funded tax payments.
    - Trust structures that freeze estate growth.

Estate taxes don't destroy their wealth — because estate exposure was minimized long before death.

Why This Is Hidden

- Estate planning is complex.

- Schools never cover generational wealth systems.

- Most attorneys focus only on wills — not full wealth engineering.

- The system profits when each generation starts over.

The reset cycle keeps the masses trapped.
The engineered system keeps the wealthy free.

The Awakening

Generational wealth isn't about leaving money — it's about leaving **control structures.**

Start now:

- Create trust structures.

- Begin financial education for heirs.

- Build family governance systems.

Without structure, wealth dies.
With structure, it compounds forever.

In the next sections, we'll break down the **specific vehicles** the ultra-rich use to legally freeze estate growth, bypass taxation, and lock control across bloodlines.

We're no longer building wealth — we're fortifying dynasties.

Trust Structures and Family Control Systems

The wealthy don't leave wealth exposed to chance.

They transfer control — not vulnerability.

Trusts and governance systems ensure that assets are protected long after the original wealth builder is gone.

Why Trusts Exist

Without trusts:

- Assets transfer directly to heirs.

- Probate courts control distribution.

- Creditors, divorces, lawsuits, and taxes can gut inheritances.

- Heirs often receive large sums they're unprepared to manage.

With trusts:

- Control stays with pre-designed rules.

- Legal insulation protects assets from external threats.

- The family vision guides wealth far beyond one generation.

The trust becomes the guardian of the dynasty.

Key Trust Structures the Wealthy Use

1. Revocable Living Trust

- Avoids probate.

- Simplifies asset transfer.

- Offers no asset protection during the grantor's lifetime.

2. Irrevocable Trust

- Removes assets from personal ownership.

- Shields assets from lawsuits and estate taxes.

- Cannot easily be altered — ensuring long-term protection.

3. Dynasty Trust

- Designed to last for multiple generations.

- Avoids repeated estate taxes.

- Preserves family control for 100+ years.

4. Asset Protection Trust (APT)

- Shields wealth from lawsuits, creditors, and legal threats.

- Often established in favorable jurisdictions for maximum protection.

Each trust serves a distinct role — together, they form a layered fortress.

The Power of the Trustee

- The trustee controls distributions according to the trust's rules.

- Co-trustees or corporate trustees maintain professional oversight.

- Beneficiaries cannot freely raid trust assets.

The wealth is not gifted — it is supervised.

This prevents:

- Reckless spending.

- Marital disputes.

- Legal threats.

- Irresponsible heirs destroying capital.

Spendthrift Clauses: The Internal Shield

- Prevents beneficiaries from assigning or pledging trust assets.

- Protects trust assets from creditors seeking repayment.

- Ensures court judgments cannot seize trust-held wealth.

Spendthrift language ensures beneficiaries cannot voluntarily or involuntarily lose the wealth.

Family Control Systems

The ultra-wealthy establish:

- **Family Constitutions** outlining values, goals, and expectations.

- **Family Councils** for collective decision-making and education.

- **Formal education plans** to train heirs in financial literacy, legal structures, and business management.

- **Philanthropic arms** to reinforce purpose and responsibility.

Control isn't forced — it's taught and maintained through cultural design.

Family Limited Partnerships (FLPs)

- Used to consolidate and manage family assets.

- Parents retain control while gifting limited partnership shares to heirs.

- Allows for valuation discounts, reducing estate tax exposure.

- Protects assets from outside legal claims.

FLPs create powerful legal and tax advantages while preserving centralized control.

The Generational Control Loop

- Assets stay in trust.

- Heirs access controlled distributions.

- Trustees enforce guidelines.

- Family governance maintains cohesion.

- Successor generations inherit not just money — but systems.

Wealth flows endlessly without triggering destructive resets.

Why This Is Rarely Discussed

- Estate law complexity discourages most people.

- Attorneys often focus on basic wills, not dynasty engineering.

- Governments prefer taxable estates and forced resets.

- Financial ignorance fuels revenue stability for the system.

The few who know — protect everything.
The rest — start over.

The Awakening

You don't need extreme wealth to begin:

- Form simple living trusts.

- Introduce family governance principles.

- Establish basic FLPs as assets grow.

Structure multiplies wealth far more than income alone.

In the next section, we'll break down the **final wealth defense system** — how the elite protect their legacy even from catastrophic legal attacks, system failures, and complete societal resets.

This is where wealth becomes nearly untouchable.

Building the Untouchable Dynasty Fortress

Most people believe no wealth is fully protected.
Lawsuits, divorces, taxes, governments, and crises can always reach it.

But the ultra-rich don't simply build wealth — they fortify it.

They create structures so deeply engineered that their wealth becomes nearly immune to attack.

The Core Concept: Legal Distance

The wealthy create **maximum legal distance** between:

- Themselves.

- Their heirs.

- Their assets.

The further wealth is separated from personal ownership, the harder it becomes to seize.

The goal is not secrecy — it's legal structure.

Multi-Jurisdictional Trust Structures

Advanced dynasty fortresses often include:

- **Domestic Asset Protection Trusts (DAPTs)** — offering strong protection within certain U.S. states (ex: Nevada, South Dakota).

- **Foreign Asset Protection Trusts (FAPTs)** — offering even stronger protection in select offshore jurisdictions (ex: Cook Islands, Nevis, Belize).

- **Hybrid Trusts** — combining domestic and foreign layers for maximum flexibility.

Offshore structures legally limit U.S. court jurisdiction, making judgments difficult to enforce internationally.

The Firewall Principle

The fortress operates with **firewalls**:

- Each entity shields the next.

- Lawsuits hit one layer but cannot pierce through others.

- Assets are held by trusts, not individuals.

- Trustees operate independently from beneficiaries.

- International diversification weakens any single government's reach.

Multiple legal barriers reduce attack surfaces dramatically.

Asset Location Diversification

The ultra-rich spread holdings across:

- Multiple banking jurisdictions.

- International real estate.

- Offshore companies.

- Hard assets stored in politically stable regions.

- Global insurance policies.

Geographic diversification ensures no single country controls the entire empire.

Political Risk Mitigation

When political climates shift:

- Domestic wealth may become vulnerable to new regulations, asset seizures, or taxation.

- International structuring insulates portions of wealth from single-government overreach.

The fortress is designed for survival — even when nations collapse.

The Role of Private Banking Relationships

Elite private banks offer:

- Discretionary management services.

- Cross-border asset protection strategies.

- Multicurrency holdings.

- Personal relationship-based lending and protections.

The wealthy don't simply "open accounts" — they build global banking alliances.

Insurance as the Final Armor

The ultra-wealthy secure:

- High-limit umbrella liability insurance.

- Key person policies.

- Political risk insurance.

- Private placement life insurance (PPLI) — a powerful tax-sheltered wealth vehicle for ultra-high-net-worth clients.

Insurance absorbs legal and financial shocks before personal or trust assets are touched.

The Dynasty Fortress Formula

Irrevocable Trusts + Multi-Jurisdictional Entities + Asset Protection Trusts + Private Banking + Insurance Layers = Untouchable Wealth Fortress

Each layer compounds legal protection:

- Lawsuits fail.

- Divorce claims fail.

- Creditors fail.

- Tax seizures fail.

- Courts struggle to pierce the system.

The deeper the structure — the harder the attack.

Why This Is Rarely Understood

- Few attorneys master these systems.

- Most financial advisors aren't trained beyond basic estate planning.

- The system profits when wealth remains exposed.

- Fear of "complexity" keeps most people passive.

The fewer people who know — the safer the system remains for the elite.

The Awakening

You don't need billions to begin:

- Start small: basic trusts, LLCs, insurance.

- Layer over time: international accounts, asset diversification.

- Build relationships: trusted legal, tax, and banking advisors.

The Dynasty Fortress isn't built overnight — but every layer moves you further from vulnerability.

In the next section, we'll conclude your forbidden training — showing how to integrate everything you've learned into a fully engineered, unbreakable personal wealth system.

You're not just building wealth anymore.
You're engineering permanent control.

Chapter 12: The Forbidden Wealth Blueprint

Installing the Complete System

You've now seen every hidden layer.

- The traps that keep the masses enslaved.

- The forbidden codes the wealthy quietly mastered.

- The structures that preserve wealth across generations.

Now we bring it all together — into one fully integrated system.

This is the blueprint the 1% use to permanently separate themselves from financial fragility.

The Three Core Phases

The ultra-wealthy operate through a simple but powerful three-phase system:

Phase 1 — Extraction Escape

- Break free from labor-based income.

- Transition from wages to ownership.

- Shift from earned income to asset-based income.

Ownership is the foundation. Labor was the trap.

Phase 2 — Structural Control

- Form legal entities (LLCs, S-Corps, Holding Companies).

- Build credit-stacked business structures.

- Use trusts to shield and direct wealth.

- Stack cash flow machines across asset classes.

Structure creates control — and control protects wealth.

Phase 3 — Perpetual Protection

- Layer multi-jurisdictional entities.
- Install asset protection trusts.
- Build Dynasty Trusts and Family Limited Partnerships.
- Activate global banking relationships.
- Implement generational wealth governance.

Protection ensures the system survives across time, politics, lawsuits, and economic collapse.

The Full Wealth Stack

Layer	Action
Income Base	Rental income, business cash flow, royalties, lending
Credit Engines	Business credit stacking, entity separation
Tax Systems	Income reclassification, entity deductions, depreciation
Legal Insulation	Trusts, FLPs, spendthrift clauses
Geographic Protection	Domestic + offshore diversification
Legacy Systems	Governance structures, family constitutions
Estate Defense	Dynasty Trusts, gifting strategies, insurance shields

Every layer feeds the next — creating unstoppable financial momentum.

The Key Principles Behind The Blueprint

- **Control matters more than ownership.**
- **Structure outperforms income.**
- **Redundancy beats prediction.**
- **Automation scales wealth beyond labor.**
- **Legal distance creates immunity.**
- **Education protects heirs from self-destruction.**

Wealth becomes a system — not a balance sheet.

Why So Few Ever Apply It

- Fear of complexity.
- Lack of financial education.
- Comfort with dependence.
- Systemic design to discourage exploration.

The knowledge has always been accessible — but never offered.

The Path Forward For You

You don't need vast capital to start.

- ☑ Build your first LLC.
- ☑ Open your first business credit lines.
- ☑ Begin small trust structures.
- ☑ Start stacking multiple income streams.
- ☑ Establish banking relationships early.
- ☑ Study advanced legal protections as wealth grows.

The earlier you build structure, the easier wealth accelerates.

The Awakening

The forbidden blueprint was never locked away — you were simply trained not to look for it.

The wealthy don't possess secret abilities.
They possess structure, knowledge, and discipline.

And now — so do you.

In the final section, we'll install the **mental operating system** the 1% run on — the psychological frame that allows this entire blueprint to function without self-sabotage or fear.

The structure is built.
Now we complete the mind that runs it.

The Wealth Operating System of the 1%

We've now engineered the external system:

- Structures.

- Entities.

- Trusts.

- Cash flow machines.

- Legal fortresses.

But none of it works without the **operating system running the mind behind it.**

Wealth isn't just a system — it's a way of thinking.

Why Most People Self-Sabotage Wealth

- Fear of complexity.

- Guilt around money.

- Programming to stay dependent.

- Scarcity-driven decisions.

- Emotional attachment to consumption.

- Inability to delay gratification.

Without mental rewiring, even great systems collapse.

The 1% install a very different frame.

Wealth Rule #1 — Control Is Priority

The masses chase:

- Income.

- Status.

- Validation.
- Consumption.

The wealthy chase:

- Control of cash flow.
- Control of taxation.
- Control of legal jurisdiction.
- Control of timing.
- Control of access.

Control creates options — and options create freedom.

Wealth Rule #2 — Delay Drives Acceleration

- The masses want fast pleasure.
- The wealthy delay gratification to multiply capital.
- Capital compounds exponentially when reinvested, not consumed.

Temporary discipline produces permanent autonomy.

Wealth Rule #3 — Systems, Not Hustle

- Labor earns.
- Systems compound.

The wealthy:

- Replace personal labor with leveraged structures.
- Build scalable systems early.
- Stack multiple income engines.

They don't work harder — they build smarter.

Wealth Rule #4 — Emotional Distance

- Money is not personal.

- Wealth-building decisions are made with clarity, not emotion.

- Fear, greed, envy, and guilt are removed from financial calculations.

Cold, rational thinking preserves capital — emotional reactions destroy it.

Wealth Rule #5 — Permanent Education

- Laws change.

- Tax codes evolve.

- Opportunities shift.

The wealthy constantly study:

- Tax law.

- Global finance.

- Asset protection strategies.

- New jurisdictions.

- Private deal flows.

They stay students of power, not victims of policy.

Wealth Rule #6 — Privacy Protects Power

- The masses chase visibility.

- The wealthy build invisibility.

They minimize:

- Public exposure.

- Personal asset registration.

- Unnecessary disclosures.

The less people know, the harder you are to attack.

Wealth Rule #7 — Legacy Over Lifestyle

The wealthy operate multi-generationally:

- Building for heirs, not just personal consumption.
- Training successors early.
- Engineering governance structures that survive their death.

They think in 100-year timelines — not yearly incomes.

The Operating System Installed

You are no longer operating on:

- Wage dependence.
- Consumer programming.
- Scarcity cycles.
- Single income risk.

You are now running:

- Ownership priority.
- Structural control.
- Legal insulation.
- Psychological resilience.
- Autonomous wealth engineering.

The forbidden system no longer controls you — you control the system.

The Final Awakening

148

The 1% don't possess magic.

They simply operate inside knowledge you were never shown.

- You now have that knowledge.

- The structure is available.

- The systems are buildable.

- The blueprint is clear.

The system was never broken — it was functioning exactly as designed.

Now you're functioning outside of it.

Final Words — Your Wealth Blacklist Is Now Activated

You've crossed a line few ever reach.

- You've seen the traps designed to keep you small.
- You've decoded the structures the elite quietly build.
- You've learned how the game is truly played.

This isn't theory anymore.
This is architecture.

You Were Never Meant To See This

The system was never broken — it was always working exactly as intended:

- To create dependency.
- To feed consumption.
- To extract labor.
- To profit from your financial ignorance.

Most remain trapped not by law — but by design.

You've now escaped that design.

The Forbidden Codes Are No Longer Forbidden

- Ownership.
- Structure.
- Credit engines.
- Legal protection.
- Tax insulation.
- Generational fortresses.

What was hidden was never truly locked — it was simply never offered.

You've now been handed what others weren't supposed to know.

The Choice Now Belongs To You

Information doesn't build wealth.

Action does.

- Form your first entity.

- Build your first asset-protected structure.

- Stack your first income machine.

- Move capital into ownership.

- Study, refine, and expand relentlessly.

Small moves compound faster than you realize.

The game begins immediately — not years from now.

You Are No Longer Dependent

- You've broken labor dependence.

- You've dismantled income fragility.

- You've stepped outside wage-based control.

- You've acquired knowledge the system prefers you never touch.

The system profits most when you delay.
You now operate without permission.

Build Quietly. Scale Aggressively. Protect Permanently.

- Do not chase visibility.

- Do not seek validation.

- Do not explain your moves to those still trapped.

This path isn't for approval.
It's for control.

Wealth is not loud.
Real wealth is engineered, protected, and invisible.

The Forbidden System Is Now Installed

- You were programmed to obey.

- You've chosen to control.

- The blueprint is no longer theoretical.

- The machine is now buildable — and unstoppable.

The Blacklist was never about exclusion.
It was your invitation.

Use it.
Build it.
Protect it.
Pass it on.

Your Wealth Blacklist is now activated.

Thank You

Thank you for choosing to step beyond what you were taught.

Most will never question the system.
Most will never see the hidden architecture behind wealth.
Most will stay exactly where the system was designed to keep them.

But you didn't.

You've now seen what few are ever shown:

- The structures.

- The leverage.

- The control.

- The operating system the 1% quietly use to build and protect power across generations.

This book was never written for the masses.
It was written for those ready to take ownership.

Use what you've learned.
Apply it with discipline.
Protect it with intention.

Your Wealth Blacklist is no longer theory.
It's now yours.

Stay quiet.
Build relentlessly.
And never surrender control.

www.ingramcontent.com/pod-product-compliance
Lightning Source LLC
Chambersburg PA
CBHW032330210326
41518CB00041B/2061